ESSENTIALS
of XBRL

Essentials Series

The Essentials Series was created for busy business advisory and corporate professionals. The books in this series were designed so that these busy professionals can quickly acquire knowledge and skills in core business areas.

Each book provides need-to-have fundamentals for those professionals who must:

- Get up to speed quickly, because they have been promoted to a new position or have broadened their responsibility scope
- Manage a new functional area
- Brush up on new developments in their area of responsibility
- Add more value to their company or clients

Other books in this series include:

For more information on any of the above titles, please visit *www.wiley.com.*

ESSENTIALS

of XBRL

*Financial Reporting
in the 21st Century*

Bryan Bergeron

WILEY

John Wiley & Sons, Inc.

For general information on our other products and services, or technical support,
please contact our Customer Care Department within the United States at
800-762-2974, outside the United States at 317-572-3993 or fax 317-572-4002.

Wiley also publishes its books in a variety of electronic formats. Some content
that appears in print may not be available in electronic books.

For more information about Wiley products, visit our web site at *www.wiley.com*.

Library of Congress Cataloging-in-Publication Data

Bergeron, Bryan P.
    Essentials of XBRL : financial reporting in the 21st century / Bryan
Bergeron.
            p. cm. — (Essentials series)
    Includes index.
        ISBN 0-471-22077-9 (pbk. : alk. paper)
    1. XBRL (Document markup language) 2. Business
enterprises—Finance—Data processing. I. Title: Financial reporting in
the 21st century. II. Title. III. Series.
    HF5548.5.X25B47 2003
        005.7'2—dc21

                                            2003006642

10 9 8 7 6 5 4 3 2 1

To Miriam Goodman

Contents

Preface

Essentials of XBRL: Financial Reporting in the 21st Century is a practical survey of the extensible business reporting language (XBRL)—a technology standard for the transparent interchange of financial and business reporting data that promises to revolutionize the financial industry. In the fast-paced world of modern business, the accurate, secure exchange of financial data has become the rate-limiting step in executing, archiving, and communicating business transactions. With XBRL, a standard based on the extensible markup language (XML), a company can seamlessly exchange financial data with other companies in near real time. In addition to intercompany communications, XBRL can be easily adopted for a variety of internal uses, from readily searchable databases to executive decision support tools.

The aim of this book is to provide an objective, vendor-independent assessment of XBRL, highlighting the positive and negative aspects of the standard. The book assumes an intelligent CEO-level reader, but one who may be unfamiliar with the challenges and significance of online financial and business reporting and needs to come up to speed in one quick reading. Although the underlying technology of XBRL is necessarily covered, the discussion is at a high level and assumes no experience with computers or network systems.

After completing this book, readers will understand how their business can benefit from products that follow the XBRL standard. Moreover, readers will be able to converse comfortably with information technology professionals regarding financial system implementation issues, understand what to look for when considering financial systems that support XBRL, and appreciate the likely ROI—and possible down-side—of embracing XBRL. To illustrate the practical aspects of XBRL in an easily digestible fashion, each chapter contains a vignette that deals with key technical, cultural, or economic issues of the technology.

Reader Return on Investment

After reading the following chapters, the reader will be able to:

- Understand how XBRL relates to similar activities in other industries and what can be learned from the successes and failures in these industries.

- Understand the technological underpinnings of XBRL and how they inherently limit the capabilities of XBRL.

- Understand the critical role XBRL can play in finance and business reporting in enabling best practices.

- Understand how XBRL can be an enabler of e-commerce.

- Understand how XBRL compares with competing standards.

- Understand the standards process and how the finance industry and the government are involved with the XBRL standard.

- Understand XBRL from historical, economic, and technical perspectives, including how it relates to the larger field of electronic data interchange (EDI).

- Have a working vocabulary of XBRL, and be able to com-municate intelligently with IT professionals and vendors regarding XBRL-compatible products and services.

- Understand the trade-offs between the commercial options available for a XBRL implementation.

- Understand the significance of XBRL on the company's bot-tom line.

- Understand the relationship between XBRL and other busi-ness optimization strategies.

- Have a set of specific recommendations that can be used to move to XBRL-based financial and business reporting.

- Appreciate the status of XBRL: what is merely promised, what exists today, and the likely status of XBRL in the future.

Organization of This Book

This book is organized into modular topics related to XBRL. It is divided into the following chapters:

Chapter 1: Overview. The first chapter provides an overview of the key concepts, terminology, and the historical context of XBRL in the finance industry. It illustrates the challenges of current business practices that XBRL is intended to address. This chapter also highlights some of the more promising alternatives to XBRL that have applicability in certain business settings.

Chapter 2: Opportunities. This chapter examines the opportunities associated with XBRL-based reporting, from perspectives of both corporate senior management and the accounting professional. It discusses the role of XBRL in providing rapid access to timely financial data to the corporation while ensuring security and accuracy.

Chapter 3: Standards. The chapter explores XBRL from the perspective of standard practices and standards organizations. Topics include traditional standard practices in the finance industry and how these relate to the new reality reporting since the advent of the Sarbanes-Oxley Act. It considers the role of vendors, the government, the general computing industry, and trade organizations in establishing standards for finance and business reporting.

Chapter 4: Process. The chapter focuses on XBRL as an enabler of financial and business process. Topics include knowledge management principles, the role of XBRL in the financial knowledge management process, the potential of XBRL beyond financial reporting, and approaches to electronic reporting.

Chapter 5: Technology. This chapter explores the technological underpinnings of XBRL, including a general discussion of markup languages, from a high-level, nontechnical perspective.

Chapter 6: Solutions. This chapter looks at the various solutions offered by vendors in the XBRL market. Topics include defining assessment metrics of performance and discussing how to prepare for and assess the impact of an XBRL initiative on the day-to-day operation of a company.

Chapter 7: Economics. The chapter explores the financial aspects of XBRL from a return-on-investment perspective. Topics include economic synergies, the burden of legacy systems, the hidden costs of XBRL, and how to justify the cost of investing in networks and other infrastructure technologies that may be necessary to support XBRL.

Chapter 8: Are We There Yet? The final chapter provides some concrete examples of the resources, time, and costs involved in embarking on a practical XBRL effort. Topics include implementation challenges, working with vendors, working within the supply chain during the transition period, realistic implementation time lines, and managing risk. This chapter ends with a critical assessment of the status of XBRL within the context of the enormous pressure on the financial industry to evolve to meet current demands of near–real-time delivery of goods and services. It differentiates between what is merely promised and what exists today and projects the evolution XBRL over the next five years.

Glossary. A short glossary is provided for the few technical terms used in this text.

Further Reading. This section lists some of the more relevant works in the area of XBRL, at a level appropriate to a CEO or upper-level manager.

How to Use This Book

For those new to online finance and business reporting, the best way to tackle the subject is simply to read each chapter in order; however, because each chapter is written as a stand-alone module, readers interested in, for example, the economics of XBRL can go directly to Chapter 7, "Economics."

Throughout the book, "In the Real World" sections provide real-world examples of how XBRL can be used to improve corporate efficiency and competitiveness. Similarly, a "Tips & Techniques" section in each chapter offers concrete steps that the reader can take to benefit from a XBRL initiative. Key terms are defined in context throughout the book. In addition, readers who want to delve deeper into the business, technical, or corporate culture aspects of XBRL are encouraged to consult the list of print and online publications listed in the "Further Reading" section.

Acknowledgments

I would like to thank my enduring editorial associate, Miriam Goodman, for her assistance is creating this work. In addition, special thanks to my managing editor at John Wiley & Sons, Sheck Cho, for his insight and encouragement.

CHAPTER 1

Overview

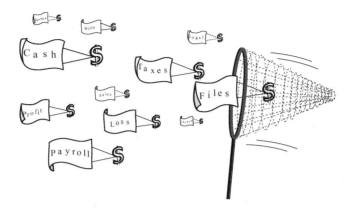

Every business is fundamentally a numbers game whose score is based on objective measures of profit, cash flow, and solvency. Moreover, keeping score—reporting—is increasingly challenging, given the complexity of the modern enterprise, with ever-changing tax rules, scrutiny from government watchdogs on corporate ethics, and the pressure from global competition. Even so, creditors, shareholders, and numerous government agencies expect to have access to accurate measures of a company's health in the form of reports that conform to generally accepted accounting principles (GAAP). These principles define how metrics, such as profit and cash flow, are calculated and reported, enabling potential investors to evaluate the relative merit of companies using a standard basis for comparison. The ability of management to create reports that reflect the true profit, cash flow, and solvency of an enterprise depends on the availability of accurate, timely data from transactions, operations, and other business-related activities throughout the enterprise. It also depends on adherence to the accounting standard.

Challenge of Reporting

To appreciate the current state of affairs in financial reporting, consider the flow of data that contributes to the financial reporting system, illustrated in Exhibit 1.1. At the start of the process, there is the creation of data by recording financial transactions and other business activities within the enterprise. Although some of these business activities may be recorded on paper, the transactions in most modern enterprises are recorded electronically. Regardless of how the transactions are recorded initially, the transaction data are entered, either automatically or by rekeying the data from paper forms into a transaction database where the data can be managed and used to generate reports.

Data from the transaction database, in either paper or electronic form, are fed to the corporate accounting database, where the data become incorporated into various accounts, schedules, files, and legal records. The accounting database serves as the basis for numerous internal and external reports. The most important external reports are the external financial

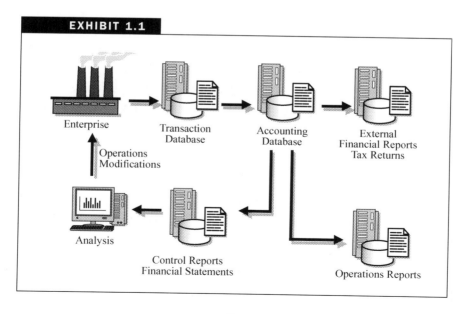

EXHIBIT 1.1

Enterprise

Transaction Database

Accounting Database

External Financial Reports Tax Returns

Operations Modifications

Analysis

Control Reports Financial Statements

Operations Reports

reports and tax returns. These reports include the income statement, cash flow statement, and balance sheet, prepared in accordance with GAAP standards and, in the case of publicly owned companies, federal security laws. The primary external tax returns are for federal and state income taxes, property taxes, sales taxes, and payroll taxes.

The internal reports, which are used by management to make decisions regarding activities such as production, investment, and hiring, include operations reports, control reports, and financial statements. Operations reports document day-to-day activity, such as payroll and sick leave. Control reports are detailed comparisons of actual versus expected results, as measured against timetables, goals, and plans. Financial statements intended for internal consumption focus on factors that drive profit, cash flow, and corporate solvency.

An analysis of the control reports and financial statements is used to identify business operations that can be improved. Exhibit 1.1 depicts an underlying process for tracking the information in the financial reporting system. For example, the original transaction data captured from the enterprise may be archived while a modified version of the data is being translated for federal tax reports.

Electronic record keeping has several advantages over paper-based methods, including shorter transaction times, lower likelihood of error, and, in most cases, lower cost per transaction. However, there are obstacles and challenges associated with moving to electronic record keeping. One of the challenges of moving from a paper-based operation to one based on electronic data interchange (EDI) is that there are several "standards" for the exchange of electronic documents. As a result, many EDI systems are not compatible with each other. To guarantee data interchange compatibility, management has to invest in EDI products from a single vendor.

A number of vendor-agnostic industry standards do exist. For example, in the healthcare industry, most clinical system vendors use the

Health Level 7 (HL7) protocol as the basis of communications. Vendors in other industries may conform to the International Telecommunications Union Telecommunications Standardization (ITU-T) standards, the American National Standards Institute (ANSI) X.12 standard, or the United Nations Electronic Data Interchange for Administration, Commerce and Transport (EDIFACT) standard, among others. In addition, the international Electronic Data Interchange Association (EDIA) works to coordinate EDI standards on a global basis.

A challenge for the management of an enterprise that uses traditional EDI systems is that sharing data with other companies or different divisions within the same company may be thwarted by groups within each enterprise that use reporting systems that adhere to their own communications standard. In addition, because there are so many "standards" from which to choose, it's likely that when one enterprise acquires another, the reporting in the acquired company may be based on a different, incompatible communications standard for its legacy systems. As a result, each reporting group within the enterprise may be forced to exchange data using paper forms. Resolving this situation requires that one of the businesses migrate to the standard used by the other part of the enterprise.

When multiple vendor-specific communications standards are used within an enterprise, integrating the different systems is generally accomplished by installing a new enterprise-wide system. Alternatively, system interfaces can be developed that allow the existing or legacy systems to share data with each other. A traditional system interface provides for the communications of data from one legacy system to another on several levels, as illustrated in Exhibit 1.2.

Traditional system interfaces allow disparate legacy systems to exchange data by providing connectivity and translation at several levels, from the low-level physical connection to the format of the data. At

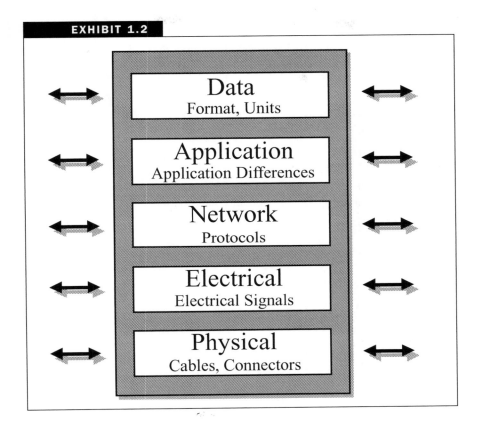

EXHIBIT 1.2

Data
Format, Units

Application
Application Differences

Network
Protocols

Electrical
Electrical Signals

Physical
Cables, Connectors

the lowest or physical level, an interface contends with issues such as differences in cables and connectors. At the next higher level, the electrical signals are translated so that they are compatible. At the network level, differences in protocols—high-level rules of how data are moved around a network—are translated. The application level of the interface handles differences in the way data are represented in particular applications. For example, the accounting system at a branch office in Milan may be different from the accounting system used at the central office in New York in terms of the type of data handled by each system. The system in Milan may not be designed to handle state taxes, for example. The highest level of an interface deals with the conversion of data formats and units. For example, the accounting system used by manage-

TIPS & TECHNIQUES

Assessing the Value of XBRL

For the average small business owner or small accounting practice, XBRL will remain invisible. One day it will simply appear as part of the upgrade to the Quicken or other accounting package. However, for managers of large corporations, major accounting firms, and the technology companies that support these firms' current financial reporting practices, XBRL deserves attention. It has the potential to greatly simplify and speed the reporting process, saving time and money.

However, before management embraces XBRL, it should have a good idea of the potential value—and potential downside—of XBRL to the organization. The key questions to ask are:

- How would converting to an XBRL-based reporting system change the day-to-day operation and management of the organization? Who are the stakeholders in such an initiative, and how would they be affected? These and related issues are discussed in Chapter 2.

- How would using an XBRL-based system support standard practices? Chapter 3 considers the role of vendors, the government, the general computing industry, and international organizations in establishing XBRL standards for finance and business reporting.

- How much could establishing a XBRL program improve the efficiency and effectiveness of the current business process? Chapter 4 discusses how XBRL relates to traditional business processes and business models.

- What tools and technologies are available for implementing XBRL, and what are their benefits and limitations? The technological aspect of XBRL, including its relation to competing standards, is discussed in Chapter 5.

ment in the Milan office may handle payroll in euros, while the accounting system in New York records payroll in U.S. dollars.

A problem with using interfaces to provide for the transfer of reporting data is that they typically allow only a subset of data to be shared between systems. In addition to the computational overhead and cost in time of translating data between systems in the two enterprises, there is the issue of the time required actually to implement the interfaces.

When data must be shared between two systems, developing or purchasing an interface designed specifically to enable data communications between the systems may be a viable solution, as in Exhibit 1.3. However, when multiple systems must share data, the number of inter-

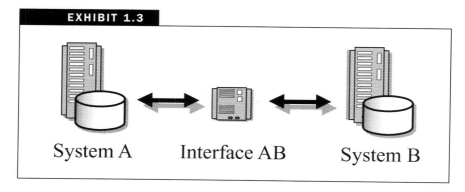

EXHIBIT 1.3

System A   Interface AB   System B

faces that must be developed to allow for the sharing of data among systems may be prohibitive. System-specific interfaces for integrating legacy systems aren't a viable solution to data communications when more than three or four systems must be connected.

For example, to provide sharing between four different systems—say a company and three recent acquisitions—six different interfaces have to be developed, as shown in Exhibit 1.4. What's more, if one of the four systems is modified or replaced, several of the interfaces may need to be modified or replaced as well. An enterprise that relies on a financial reporting system built around multiple EDI standards and multiple, system-specific interfaces relies on a moving target. Such a system is typically perpetually in development.

Enter the Web

As one of the major disruptive technologies of the 20th century, the web changed everything. With the success of the Internet as a conduit for e-commerce, e-mail, and general communications, the language used to make static Web pages, Hypertext Markup Language (HTML), became a de facto standard virtually overnight. However, when companies began to explore sharing transaction data in real time instead of simply creating online brochures, developers looked elsewhere. As a result, several languages were developed to allow integration of databases over the Internet. One of these languages, XML (eXtensible Markup

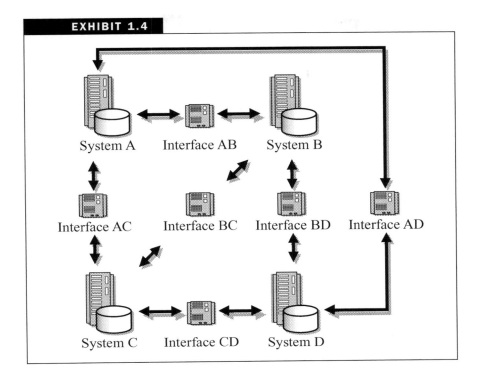

EXHIBIT 1.4

Language), a relative of HTML, is rapidly gaining in popularity in the information technology community.

XML's popularity stems from several of its key characteristics. Perhaps most important, the language is compatible with the Internet. As a result, vendors developing software that uses the web (a graphical interface to the Internet) for communications can make several important assumptions. One assumption is that the environment is greatly simplified, so that a vendor developing a system that provides connectivity between computer systems need be concerned only with the format of data and differences in applications (see Exhibit 1.5) and can ignore the physical, electrical, and network components of data communications. Furthermore, in most cases, the application differences are simply the small differences in the Web browsers provided by Microsoft and Netscape.

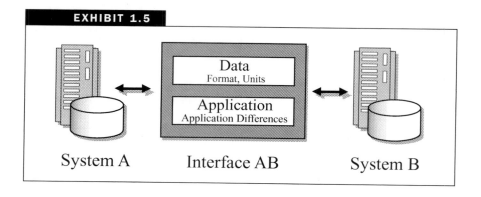

EXHIBIT 1.5

Data
Format, Units

Application
Application Differences

System A   Interface AB   System B

XML is gaining support across every industry that relies on e-commerce and on the Internet for communications. In addition, as its name suggests, XML is extensible, or easily modified. Its vocabulary can be extended to include virtually any type of text or image data, in any field. This ease of modification translates to cost savings for vendors creating interfaces between systems. Another characteristic of XML that is attractive to the development community and corporate information technology (IT) community is that the language is freely available and not tied to a particular vendor. However, the lack of a vendor backing the language has a number of repercussions, as discussed in more detail in Chapter 3.

One of the evolving extensions or evolutions of XML is the eXtensible Business Reporting Language (XBRL). What makes XBRL different from generic XML is that the XBRL vocabulary is established by standards committees. In contrast, XML is a language—not a standard. Using the standard XBRL vocabulary, business transactions and operations can be referred and reported in a standard way.

Reporting systems that communicate with each other through a common XML-based standard, such as XBRL, are much less complex than those communicating through multiple, dedicated interfaces. The use of XBRL also simplifies the challenge of integrating disparate

IN THE REAL WORLD

Establishing XBRL as a Standard

The movement to establish the XBRL as a standard for the preparation and exchange of financial reports and data was spearheaded by the American Institute of Certified Public Accountants and approximately 30 other organizations. Since the first XBRL steering committee meeting in 1999, the list of participants has expanded to include prominent financial institutions, professional service organizations, technology enablers, accounting and trade organizations, and a number of formal liaisons and alliances. A partial list of those organizations active in the XBRL Steering Committee that offer products and services related to XBRL includes:

Adobe

AICPA

Association of Investment Management Researchers

Australia Prudential Regulatory Authority

Beckon Microparts

Borland

Bridge News

Caseware

CICA

Cogniant, Inc.

CPA Australia

Creative Solutions

Crowe Chizek

Deloitte & Touche, LLP

Deutsche Bundesbank

Dow Jones & Co., Inc.

e-Content company

Edgar Online

Epicor Software Corp.

Ernst & Young, LLP

Federal Deposit Insurance Corporation

Fidelity Investments

Financial Accounting Standards Board

Financial Executives International

FRx Software Corporation

Fujitsu

General Electric Company

Grant Thornton

Great Plains

Hitachi

Hyperion

IN THE REAL WORLD CONTINUED

IASC	Practitioners Publishing
IBM	Company
ICAEW	PricewaterhouseCoopers
IMA	Reuters Group LP
J.D. Edwards & Co.	Sage
JP Morgan & Co., Inc.	SAP AG
KPMG International	Securities and Exchange
Lawson	Commission
Microsoft	Standard and Poor's
Moody's Risk Management	Standards Committee Germany
Services, Inc.	Sun Microsystems
Morgan Stanley Dean Witter	Thomson Financial
Multex.com, Inc.	Tokyo Shoho Research
Nasdaq	Toshiba
Navision Software	U.S. Census
NEC	U.S. Department of Defense
NetLedger	UBMatrix
New River	University of Kansas
NTT Data	The Woodburn Group
Oinke, Inc.	XBRLSolutions, Inc.
Oracle	XML Consortium Japan
PeopleSoft	

In addition, there are similar XML-based initiatives in virtually every industry that is dependent on sharing data across the Internet or other network.

reporting systems. As illustrated in Exhibit 1.6, each system to be integrated needs only to be compatible with the XBRL standard in order to be compatible with each other. Communications over the Internet

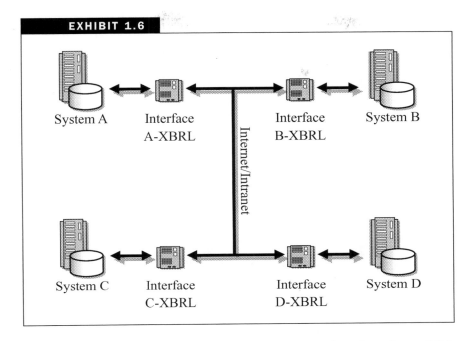

EXHIBIT 1.6

System A   Interface   Interface   System B
            A-XBRL   B-XBRL

                    Internet/Intranet

System C   Interface   Interface   System D
            C-XBRL   D-XBRL

that are based on XML or a derivative are commonly referred to as Web Services.

Payoff

At first glance, the profound advantages of a simplified, Internet-based integration scheme for the financial reporting industry may not be readily apparent. To illustrate the advantages, let's return to the examination of financial reporting data in an enterprise. However, instead of the system of multiple databases and applications passing printed and electronic reports from one system to the next, each with a different format or level of detail, a single document is used for all reporting activity, as in Exhibit 1.7.

Compared with the traditional method of financial reporting, the Internet-based solution has a number of advantages. The most obvious is simplification. Instead of multiple databases, each storing and forwarding data to other systems, there is a central accounting database that stores the reporting data. Another advantage of this system is that the data flow is inherently parallel, instead of sequential as in Exhibit 1.1. As a result, throughput is increased.

A major advantage of Internet-based reporting that isn't evident in Exhibit 1.7 is that financial information from transactions and other business activities is maintained on a single XBRL document, maintained (in this example) in the Accounting Database. This one document can be accessed by operations, printed for an annual report, accessed by federal agencies, imported into other databases, or published on the web. Furthermore, in each instance, what the user or agency sees in terms of content, granularity, and formatting is appropriate to its needs. Furthermore, assuming everyone is using the XBRL standard, off-the-shelf software, such as Microsoft Access and Microsoft Excel, can be used to access the document.

In all, this translates to time and cost savings for finance and accounting professionals. Instead of employing staff to create financial statements for every user in the financial reporting chain, only one doc-

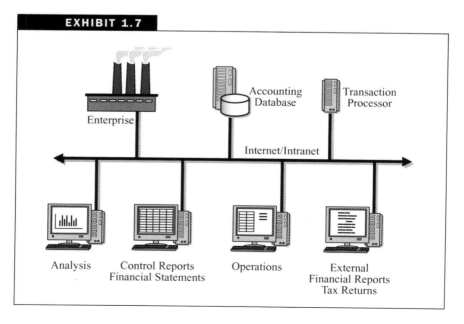

EXHIBIT 1.7

ument need be created. Furthermore, because everyone is using the Internet, there is no rekeying of data and only minimal use of paper reports, other than for archival purposes. There needn't be dedicated applications for analysis and operations, because these can be centralized and accessed over the Internet as well. In addition, because geographical location is irrelevant on the Internet, the main office of the enterprise may be located in Taiwan, the operations staff may be in Detroit, and the management team dedicated to analysis may be in New York.

Consider the advantages of such a system to the general financial community. For the information aggregators, the system facilitates the collection, aggregation, and publishing of the financial results of publicly held companies. Investment analysts can quickly and easily compare financial statements from different companies. With access to the reports of hundreds of companies at their fingertips, financial aggregators can analyze more financial data with greater efficiency.

Although other standards could be used with the Internet to make all of this possible, XBRL has several features that make it an obvious choice in the modern Internet-enabled corporate environment. However, before delving into these features, a definition of XBRL is in order.

Definition

A complete definition of the eXtensible Business Reporting Language is inherently technical in nature. However, for the purpose of this book, it is defined from a practical business perspective in this way:

> eXtensible Business Reporting Language (XBRL) is an open, platform-independent, international standard for the timely, accurate, efficient, and cost-effective electronic storage, manipulation, repurposing, and communication of financial and business reporting data.

From this definition, it should be clear that XBRL is fundamentally about a *standard* language for *reporting* financial data. In this context, a standard is an agreed-upon principle of protocol. Standards are set by committees working under various trade and international organizations. In the U.S. financial industry, the key standards organization involved with establishing XBRL standards is the American Institute of Certified Public Accountants (AICPA). XBRL is an *international* standard because of the involvement of financial standards organizations around the world, including the international financial standards organizations listed in Exhibit 1.8. In today's environment of multinational companies, limiting XBRL to a single country isn't feasible, because it would simply create another layer of complexity in the overall financial and business reporting process.

XBRL is a *language,* in that it is a system of communicating with its own set of special words. As the name suggests, the XBRL is a language concerned with communicating words that deal with *business* reporting. In other words, it isn't a universal language but is optimized for the needs of the business community. Although XBRL is a *reporting* language, its uses extend beyond simple financial reporting.

As an extension of XML, XBRL is itself an *extensible* language, meaning that its vocabulary can be easily modified to suit the changing needs of the finance industry. For example, new words can be added to

EXHIBIT 1.8

ACRONYM	INTERNATIONAL FINANCIAL STANDARDS ORGANIZATIONS
CICA	Chartered Accountants of Canada
CGA	Certified General Accountants (Canada)
ICAA	Institute of Chartered Accountants in Australia
CPA	Certified Public Accountants of Australia
HKSA	Hong Kong Society of Accountants
IASB	International Accounting Standards Board
IFAC	International Federation of accountants
ICA	Institute of Chartered Accountants in Ireland
ICAEW	Institute of Chartered Accountants in England and Wales
NIVRA	Netherlands Institute of Registered Accountants

support communications regarding a new federal tax in the United States or a new payroll deduction in the European Union.

As an illustration of the parallels between XML and XBRL, consider that the English language, as defined by the *Encarta Dictionary*, is to the English language as defined in *Barron's Dictionary of Business Terms* as XML is to XBRL. Similarly, there are dialects of XML in use or in development in the medical and legal professions, in engineering, and in business (see Exhibit 1.9), just as there are specialized dictionaries for these and other areas of specialization.

XML can be considered a superset of XBRL, just as the *Encarta Dictionary* might have multiple definitions for a given word, one for each context in which the word may be used, whereas *Barron's* typically has one or, less frequently, two definitions for the same word. For example, there are 39 definitions for "stock" in the *Encarta dictionary*, from "the frame of a horse-drawn plow" to "movie film that has not yet been

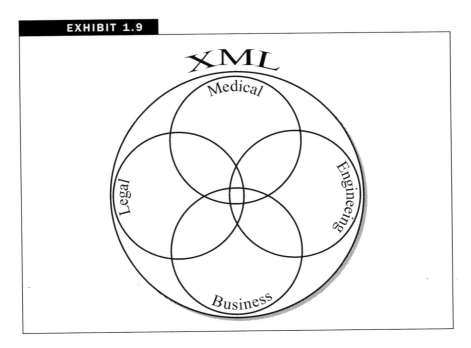

EXHIBIT 1.9

exposed." In contrast, *Barron's* lists only two definitions, one from the perspective of inventory and the other with ownership of a company. Just as the editors of *Barron's Dictionary of Business Terms* decide which words belong in their dictionary, the various standards committees decide which words can be incorporated into XBRL.

Although virtually any language can be extended by adding new words to the language, the key is the ease with which XBRL can be extended. In fact, XBRL is so easy to extend that a real danger is the potential of a veritable tower of Babel that could result from every major financial institution adding words that address its internal needs but that aren't acceptable to the national and international standards organizations. The implications of easy extensibility are considered in depth in Chapter 3.

Even though XBRL has backing from Microsoft, IBM, Adobe, Sun Microsystems, and other industry leaders, it is a nonproprietary, *open* language. As a result, the definitions within the XBRL standard are freely available. This is in contrast with a proprietary language, in which the definitions of underlying words may be unpublished and, for all practical purposes, unavailable. An advantage of this openness is that vendors, customers, and the standards bodies all have free access to the definitions. As a result, there should be minimal confusion over word definitions and less room for error.

Another characteristic of XBRL that it inherits from XML is that it is *platform independent*. Just as English is the accepted language of business for most of the world, XML runs on all of the major computer hardware under the most common operating systems. By extension, XBRL runs on hardware from Dell, Sun Microsystems, Hewlett-Packard, Apple Computer, Compaq, and IBM, under operating systems from UNIX and Linux to Microsoft Windows.

XBRL, like other markup languages, associates nonprintable characters and words with data. For example, as shown in Exhibit 1.10, whereas the traditional communications of a value for, say, payroll,

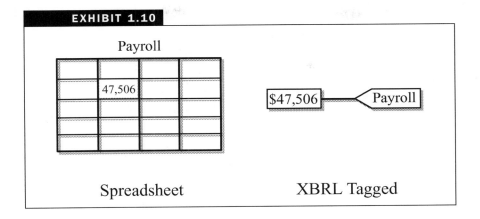

EXHIBIT 1.10

Payroll

47,506

$47,506 — Payroll

Spreadsheet   XBRL Tagged

would appear as plain text, in XBRL the tag "Payroll" would be attached to the value. The significance of the value in the spreadsheet depends on its position. The XBRL tagged data has meaning that is independent of its location in a spreadsheet, database, or any other application. For the curious reader, the actual XML statement for the tagged payroll value appears as:

```
<Payroll currency="US Dollars">47,506</Payroll>
```

In other words, the payroll is $47,506, in U.S. dollars. This simple association of the tag with the value gives XBRL several important advantages over traditional methods of communicating data from one system to another.

As an illustration of the utility of tagged data, consider a historical perspective on how products are handled in a typical grocery store. Prior to the development of the bar code—a series of vertical lines or bars used to assign a unique identification code to an item—and the standardization of the bar code "language" for the retail industry in the 1970s, grocery store owners had only a few options in identifying the price of an item on the store shelves. They could place a price list on a board, list prices on cards attached to the location on the shelves corresponding to where the goods are stocked, or directly label the individual items.

Labeling the individual items is a major improvement over simply marking the bin for the customer. Customers don't have to write down the price of each item so that they can be certain that they aren't overcharged by the checkout clerk. For clerks, affixing the price to each item frees them from having to remember the price of every item or from taking the time to look up prices on a price list.

With a bar code reader and products labeled with bar codes corresponding to the Uniform Product Code (UPC), it's possible to bypass the manual keying of prices, thereby avoiding a major source of error and speeding the checkout process. Moreover, when integrated with EDI and a database system, a bar code reader system enters the price of the item in the cash register, deducts the items from inventory, records the time and date of the transaction, and may send a message to the central office to send more of the product. With the standard bar code system, the entire checkout process is more accurate, efficient, and, in most cases, cost effective.

As an example of a challenge associated with traditional EDI systems, consider that although the UPC/bar code system is the standard for retail items throughout much of the world, some other countries use other standards. For example, the EAN (European Article Number) is used in the EU, and the JAN (Japanese Article Number) is used in Japan. Other bar code systems that are used with EDI, such as the ISBN (International Standard Book Number) system, which is used as an index to identify a book's author, title, country of origin, publisher, and price at the checkout counter, are universal.

Just as the UPC and bar code transformed the retail grocery business, XBRL is positioned to transform the financial reporting business by providing more timely, accurate, efficient, cost-effective reporting. Just as a UPC bar code allows every item to be automatically entered into the checkout register in a grocery store, every piece of financial transaction data stored in XBRL format needn't be manually rekeyed. As long as the systems all communicate via the same dialect of XBRL, there are no keying errors and data are transferred from one system to the next at near the speed of light. Cost savings derive from not having to pay for rekeying of data from paper into a computer system and time savings resulting from virtually instantaneous communications of financial data.

Using an XBRL-based system involves added overhead just as the UPC/bar code system added overhead to grocery transactions, but with enough volume, this overhead is more than offset by the cost savings. This relationship between volume and cost savings is illustrated in Exhibit 1.11, which shows that the overhead of using XBRL over nontagged data, in terms of the cost per data element due to extra storage capacity and processing requirements, is more than offset with sufficient reporting volume. This relationship is described more fully in Chapter 7.

The data expressed in XBRL aren't necessarily earmarked for interdepartmental, business-to-business, or business-to-government communications but may be analyzed, formatted, and otherwise manipulated locally for a variety of purposes. The data also may be archived for

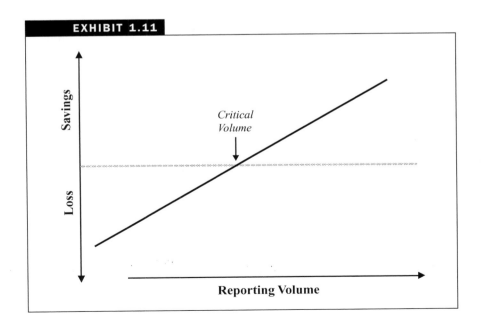

EXHIBIT 1.11

repurposing in the future. XBRL facilitates these uses as well. For example, in preparing graphics of payroll taxes for a stockholders' meeting, it isn't necessary to know the exact location of all payroll tax data within a database but merely that data tagged as "sales tax" is collected and repurposed for the presentation.

Thus far, the discussion has centered on financial data, which can be interpreted in a variety of ways. However, for discussing more of the merits of XBRL, these definitions and concepts apply:

- *Data* are numbers. They are numerical quantities derived from transactions or calculations.

- *Information* is data in context. Information is a collection of data and associated explanations, interpretations, and other textual material concerning a particular object, event, or process.

- *Metadata* is data about information. Metadata includes descriptive summaries and high-level categorization of data and information. That is, metadata is information about the context in which information is used.

- *Knowledge* is information that is organized, synthesized, or summarized to enhance comprehension, awareness, or understanding. Knowledge is a combination of metadata and an awareness of the context in which the metadata can be applied successfully.

As shown in Exhibit 1.12, the concepts defining knowledge are related hierarchically, with data at the bottom of the hierarchy and knowledge at the top. In general, each level up the hierarchy involves greater contextual richness. For example, in finance, the hierarchy could appear as:

- *Data:* $47,506

- *Information:* Payroll: $47,506

- *Metadata:* Payroll subject to State Tax: $40,232

- *Knowledge:* The corporation can decrease the state tax by moving the main production facility to another state.

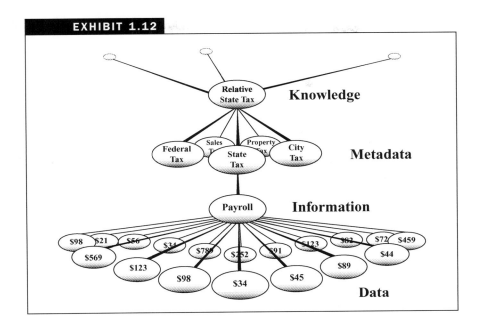

EXHIBIT 1.12

In this example, the data are simple numerical values with no real meaning out of context. However, when the value is tagged with "Payroll," it becomes information, in that it can be analyzed more readily in the context of business reporting. Analysis in the context of the state tax rules reveals an even richer context (metadata). A senior manager who is aware of the tax laws in other states is aware of the tax rate relative to other states (knowledge). In other words, knowledge is a form of human awareness based on heuristics or rules of thumb that provide contextual information. The distinction among data, information, and metadata will become more important in the discussion of process in Chapter 4.

Reality Check

A reporting system based on the XBRL standard has the potential to improve the efficiency of corporate reporting practices, thereby allowing management to focus corporate resources on its core competency.

However, even though the reporting industry appears to be embracing XBRL as a communications standard, it is by no means a panacea. The major challenges associated with XBRL are outlined here and discussed throughout the remaining chapters.

- *XBRL is a language, not a process.* The concept of an industry-wide standard for financial reporting has obvious benefits to corporations and their shareholders. However, XBRL—or any other language—is only one component in what must be an industry-wide process that supports best practices. Even though XBRL has many features that appear to make it an ideal vehicle for process improvement, other languages and other technologies could be applied to the process.

- *XBRL, as a standard, has a finite life span.* Every standard has a finite life span. A major issue in deciding whether and when to invest in XBRL-based reporting is the longevity of the standard. Many standards in the computer industry—especially those related to the Internet—reach maturity and enter decline before much of the industry has had a chance to embrace them. Furthermore, as standards go, XBRL is relatively immature and will likely continue to evolve over the next several years.

- *Underlying technology isn't perfect—yet.* XBRL and other derivatives of XML are viewed by many in the information technology world as the wave of the future. However, XBRL isn't without its shortcomings and unknowns. There are issues of security and questions about whether new Internet initiatives based on XML, such as Web services, will be successful. Furthermore, competing technologies, including other flavors of XML, threaten the position of XBRL as the lingua franca of the financial and business communities.

- *Information technology is in flux.* In the computer industry, the only constant is change. The industry has witnessed several sweeping waves of change, from centralized, mainframe-based computing to PC (personal computer)-based distributed, client-server computing, to web-based computing. Furthermore, each change has brought with it new business practices. For example, the electronic spreadsheet, made possible by the PC, revolutionized the accounting industry. It's likely that the next wave of change, such as Grid computing, where computing power as well as data are distributed over a network, or wireless computing, which allows for real-time data collection from radio-frequency identification tags, will bring change to business practices. Inevitably, XBRL will be regarded as a legacy system that the financial industry will have to deal with.

- *Change takes time.* Realistic implementation times for developing a workable XBRL-based reporting system range from a few months to a year or more, depending on the complexity of the current reporting processes, the size and geographical extent of the company, and the rate of change in the general reporting industry.

- *Capital requirements may be significant.* Business as usual doesn't require any additional investment. However, investing in what can be future gains in reporting efficiency and related cost savings may require significant capital. New system development requires time and effort from programmers, IT support staff, and travel for company representatives to attend XBRL-related conferences and working group meetings.

- *Legacy systems may require a long-term commitment.* It may not be possible to escape the responsibility of supporting legacy reporting systems for years to come. Even if a multinational corporation is capable of moving to an XBRL-based reporting system in one sweeping move, inevitable acquisitions and mergers will likely require management to deal with reporting systems that aren't XBRL-compatible. Furthermore, there may be no immediate migration path to an XBRL-based system. For example, if a U.S. company acquires a company in Asia, no XBRL-compatible reporting system that supports local and

U.S. financial reporting requirements may exist. As a result, management in the U.S. corporate office must make provision for working with the newly acquired legacy system while supporting the main XBRL-based reporting system.

Whether moving to a reporting system based on XBRL makes sense for a particular corporation depends on the business, the reporting volume, the likely return on investment, and management's aversion to risk. The following chapters are designed to help the reader assess the implications of developing or otherwise investing in XBRL-based reporting from the perspectives of technology, the reporting industry, and the economics of the proposition.

Summary

Financial reporting in the modern corporate environment is a complex, ever-changing process that stands to benefit from an industry-wide standard for electronic communications of financial reporting data. XBRL is positioned as the major technological solution to providing continuity throughout the reporting chain because it has major industry, government, and vendor backing and because the core technology, eXtensible Markup Language (XML), is gaining wide acceptance throughout the information technology community as the primary means of providing efficient data communications over the Internet.

The issue for the management of corporations with significant reporting volume is whether to invest in XBRL now or take a wait-and-see approach. Although there is risk in joining the other first movers in embracing the technology, the potential downside of waiting for the majority of the industry to move to XBRL is missing out on the cost savings, greater efficiency, and other competitive advantages that the technology promises.

A wonderful harmony is created when we join together the seemingly unconnected.

—Heraclitus

CHAPTER 2

Opportunities

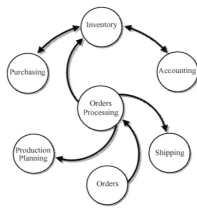

After reading this chapter you will be able to

- Appreciate the opportunities that XBRL-based financial and business reporting represents to the accounting profession

- Understand the critical role XBRL can play in finance and business reporting in enabling best practices

- Understand the relationship between XBRL and traditional electronic data interchange (EDI)

- Appreciate the value to the corporation of timely, secure access to accurate financial data

X BRL is positioned as a disruptive technology for corporate accountants and accounting firms in that it has the capacity to change the accounting profession profoundly. Just as the introduction of the electronic spreadsheet redefined the personal accounting industry and the way top accounting firms do business, XBRL-based reporting has the potential to transform accounting practices at all levels, from a fee-for-service to a consultation relationship.

This chapter continues with the exploration of XBRL as a reporting language as introduced in Chapter 1 and moves to examine the opportunities associated with the language, from the perspectives of corporate senior management and the accounting professional. As a basis for discussing these and related issues, consider this scenario, which illustrates the benefit of XBRL-based reporting for two companies and their respective accounting firms: a small company, ATI, Inc., and a Fortune 1000 company, Conglomerate, Inc. ATI is an 18-employee C corporation and a customer of CD & Associates, a small accounting firm.

Back to the Future

CD & Associates employs four certified public accountants (CPAs), an attorney, a receptionist, and four administrative assistants. In addition, during the busy corporate tax filing season, several consultant accountants and administrative assistants are hired to fill the anticipated need for additional support. The accounting practice caters primarily to small companies located near the firm with fewer than 100 employees. It also occasionally prepares the personal income tax for the executives of those corporations. Everyone in the practice is connected to a network-based accounting program that is used to prepare the corporate returns and provide other filing services for the firm's customers.

ATI, Inc., is a typical CD customer. It relies on CD & Associates for federal and state filing and a separate payroll service company to handle payroll and the related reporting for its employees. Every year, about six weeks prior to the corporate filing deadline, a representative from ATI delivers the general ledger and other financial reports printed from its in-house accounting program. Even though the data are managed in electronic form, they are in a format that is incompatible with the accounting firm's software package. As a result, ATI's administrative assistants are tasked with the time-consuming, error-prone task of rekeying the data into a second accounting program.

TIPS & TECHNIQUES

Hands–on Experience

Microsoft was the first technology company to report financials in XBRL format. Readers who want to experience some of the potential benefits of XBRL-based reporting firsthand can go to Microsoft's website (*www.Microsoft.com/msft/tools.htm*) and use the library of XBRL on the site for analysis of the data. Microsoft's XBRL site offers a Financial History PivotTable and what-if analysis programs, initial public offering investment tools, and investor stock information tools, all based on XBRL-formatted data. In addition to the tools, which are fully functional over the web, Microsoft's financials can be downloaded in XBRL format.

XBRL financial data and numerous utilities are posted on the XBRL website (*www.xbrl.com*). Several major IT vendors have XBRL demonstration sites as well. For example, IBM offers a free XML utility that enables an application to read and write data (*www.alphaworks.ibm.com/tech/xml4j*). Oracle provides a similar software package for use with its Oracle database (*otn.oracle.com/tech/xml/content.html*). Sun's website lists an extensive library of utilities for manipulating XML documents (*java.sun.com/xml/index.html*). James Clark's website provides links to XML example data and utilities (*http://jclark.com/xml/*).

In addition to the potential of introducing errors into the reporting data through manual rekeying, there are several other limitations associated with ATI's financial reporting process. For example, inevitably, two weeks prior to the filing deadline, one of the assistants in the accounting firm discovers that some critical data are missing—a bank statement, for example. Because it's near the corporate filing deadline, the bank service center is backlogged with requests for copies of statements from other companies, and it can't provide copies of the printed statements prior to the filing deadline. As a result, CD & Associates files for an extension on ATI's behalf, with checks attached for the estimated tax payments. About a month later, the tax return is completed, usually—but not always—without a penalty for underpayment of estimated taxes.

In this scenario, illustrated in Exhibit 2.1, ATI uses an internal, part-time accountant to keep the books for internal records and to provide reports that senior management uses to monitor expenses and make business projections from one quarter to the next. Paper-based data exchange is the primary method of data sharing, despite internal computerization of accounting and payroll functions by the respective services. ATI's management looks to CD & Associates primarily for assur-

EXHIBIT 2.1

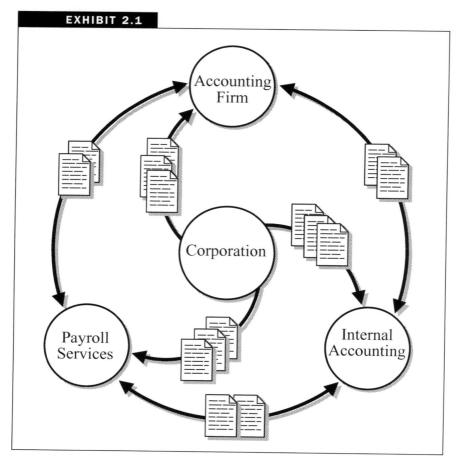

ance that it's fulfilling state and federal guidelines for reporting. The accounting practice also verifies that the payroll service is dispersing funds properly and that federal and state filings are correct and timely.

Now let's look ahead to a time when XBRL-based reporting over the Internet is the norm. Exhibit 2.2 depicts a possible scenario for financial reporting data flow for a corporation with Internet-based XBRL-enabled reporting that is provided by a small accounting firm. There are no paper reports to exchange or rekey. The administrative assistant at ATI once charged with entering financials into a proprietary accounting program now uses a web-based accounting package main-

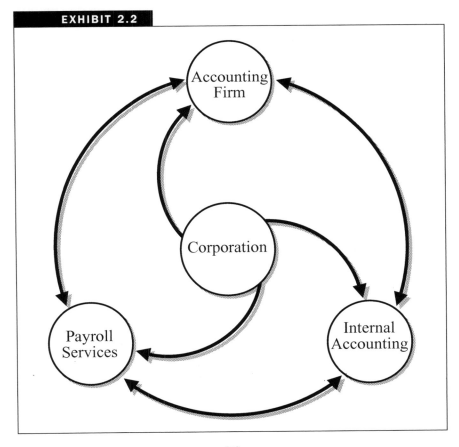

EXHIBIT 2.2

tained and served by CD & Associates. In this model, ATI staff and management enter and view financial reports through any personal computer (PC) in the company—or at home—running a Web browser, such as Microsoft Explorer. Management can also view near–real-time reports on the corporate status while traveling or when otherwise away from a PC connected to the Internet, using wireless Web devices, such as wireless PDAs (personal digital assistants).

In this scenario, no paper documents are ferried between ATI and the bank or federal or state agencies. Instead, government agencies review ATI's financial reports by accessing an XBRL document maintained on CD & Associates' *server*. Even though the agencies and ATI's management view the same document, it's rendered on their computer screens at a level of detail and in a format that each requires for reporting. Similarly, the XBRL document, which also serves as a repository for payroll activity, is routinely accessed by the appropriate governmental agencies, also in their preferred format and level of detail.

Because the digital XBRL document describing ATI's financials is updated on a daily basis, CD & Associates doesn't have to brace for the big rush just prior to the filing deadlines or hire additional help every year near the filing deadline. ATI doesn't have to contend with the uncertainty of whether it has all of its records in place near tax preparation time, since the bank and payroll service update the XBRL document on CD & Associates' server. Not only is the reporting process streamlined, but duplication of effort is eliminated, and there is no need for the accounting firm, the bank, or federal and state tax offices to hire extra data entry personnel to duplicate the data ATI personnel have already entered.

As a professional service organization, CD & Associates has been transformed from a data collection, processing, and formatting service to an electronic data repository and application service provider (ASP). The firm provides ATI with access to locally maintained accounting software, which automatically updates a single XBRL document that serves the reporting needs of ATI's management and the various reporting agencies.

Furthermore, because updates to accounting rules can be communicated directly to CD & Associates from the Internal Revenue Service (IRS) and other government agencies, the firm can operate with fewer employees. In addition, the firm's accountants take advantage of the revenue-generating potential of their personal relationship with the management of ATI. The accountants take on much more of a consultative role, offering ATI management a variety of custom reports and the interpretation that suit its particular needs.

In this new paradigm, made possible by access to virtually real-time reporting, CD & Associates provides higher value-added services to ATI, beyond simply ensuring compliance with reporting requirements. To fulfill this role, the four accountants acquired additional training in areas such as forecasting and data analysis. Buoyed by its success in its new role, CD & Associates expands its employee base to include more higher-level accountants with training in management, decision support, and information technology.

One of ATI's major customers is Conglomerate, Inc., a multinational Fortune 1000 corporation with over 100 subsidiaries and offices distributed throughout the world. ATI and Conglomerate communicate through Conglomerate's proprietary paperless electronic data interchange (EDI) system that handles orders, invoices, and other product-related business.

For its reporting responsibilities, Conglomerate employs an army of accountants that is constantly operating in emergency mode, racing from one reporting deadline to the next. Management is typically 60 days or more behind transaction postings. As such, its assessment of cash flow, liquidity, and profit lags the actual values by two months or more. In addition, the central accounting office deals with language translation and currency conversions as well as regional variations in tax rates and payroll laws. There are also several banks and payroll services involved in supporting the operation of each supplier. As illustrated in Exhibit 2.3, the buyer (left) uses an EDI system for business transactions (solid lines) with its suppliers. One supplier (right) has an additional XBRL-based reporting system (dashed line) to handle its financial reporting.

For the past two decades, Conglomerate, Inc. has been heavily reliant on an EDI system to provide paperless communications to its thousands of suppliers. It issues orders, makes payments, and handles all related business transactions with suppliers electronically. Because Conglomerate controls so much of its market, any supplier that wants to do business with Conglomerate has to become part of its proprietary EDI system. In spite of the expense of installing the system, many small suppliers make the investment in the EDI system to become part of Conglomerate's lucrative supply chain.

EXHIBIT 2.3

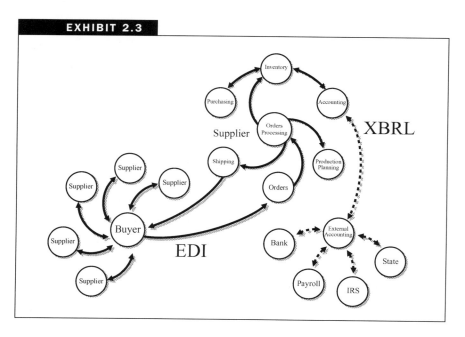

IN THE REAL WORLD

Babel versus Byzantines

A key feature of XML is its extensibility, meaning that new tags can be added easily to suit the needs of a particular business or industry. However, as a standard, extensibility isn't necessarily desirable. There are hundreds of XML-based "standard" languages in areas from medicine to the military. In this regard, XBRL could be considered simply one more of the many industry-specific languages with which companies agree to exchange business messages.

One way to avoid a veritable Tower of Babel is to involve standards organizations that extend beyond a particular industry. For example, committees for the more general ebXML and the finance-focused XBRL have cross-communications to coordinate their activities. ebXML has a much broader mission than XBRL, in that it is industry neutral, whereas XBRL is aimed expressly at the financial reporting industry. There are also important differences in the application of the two languages, in the ebXML is transaction oriented, whereas XBRL is concerned with historical reporting.

Independent languages, each optimized for a specific purpose and based on different standards, aren't necessarily a deterrent to progress. A language that provides everything for everyone is typically bloated, unwieldy, and difficult to maintain. Furthermore, if multiple committees and industry groups must agree on the vocabulary of the language, progress in evolving the standards to meet new needs is considerably slowed.

From a systems implementation perspective, what's more important for IT professionals is that the mix of systems used by an organization is compatible in terms of platform requirements, network performance, security measures, and other components. For example, a corporation can employ ebXML-based systems for transactions and XBRL-based reporting. There is synergy because both systems use the same hardware and software platform and both run on a Web browser environment that can be easily maintained.

The management of Conglomerate relies on BigFive, one of the top international accounting firms. BigFive uses its own proprietary EDI system to collect accounting data from each of Conglomerate's subsidiaries and offices, and has its staff rekey many of the reports destined for government consumption. When BigFive approaches the management of Conglomerate regarding the possibility of moving to XBRL-based reporting, it isn't an easy sell. Within Conglomerate, the primary opposition is from the head of information services (IS), who is considering migrating the current EDI system to one based on an XML-based system, such as ebXML (electronic business XML), because it would be easier to manage and would demand fewer IS resources to maintain. As the 800-pound gorilla of its industry, Conglomerate is also considering developing its own XML-based standard that its network of suppliers would have to adopt.

The director of information technology (IT) discourages corporate management from moving to XBRL or any other emerging technology until it proves viable in the marketplace and technically solid. For example, XBRL over the Internet presents security risks that most EDI systems do not. The director of IT is also considering developing a pilot program to test the viability of ebXML and other alternatives to the aging but workable EDI system. When the company does move to a new financial reporting system, the head of IT wants it to be compatible with the infrastructure used for other communications within the corporation and between the corporation and its suppliers. In the end, the management of Conglomerate, Inc. decides to take a wait-and-see approach in committing resources to an XBRL implementation.

The contrast in the approaches to business reporting taken by the managements of ATI and Conglomerate illustrates several key issues relating to the size of the corporation, parallel developments in EDI, opportunities for accounting professionals, the reporting value chain, and the underlying business model. These issues are described in detail below.

Opportunities

XBRL is fundamentally about efficient information sharing with increased speed and efficiency. It's also about enhanced distribution and rapid analysis of business data. XBRL supports innovations that can magnify the payoff that results from this enhanced communications capability. The potential payoff of moving to XBRL reporting is a function of whether the current reporting practice is paper or computer based. For the accounting professional, the benefits of computerizing a paper-based practice are obvious: fewer errors of omission and commission, potentially lower cost (depending on reporting volume), and a computing infrastructure that can be used to perform additional analysis and provide customers with services beyond basic reporting.

For the corporate manager, the payoff of moving to XBRL-based reporting is predominantly in the timely access to business intelligence and the ability to use a variety of web-enabled tools to help in making operational decisions. These tools can be used to compare, for example, the performance of public companies in the same market. Using Microsoft's XBRL-enabled Office suite of tools, including the Excel spreadsheet and Access database applications, managers have the ability to take in near–real-time data from their operations and perform what-if analysis, graph the results, and save the analysis for future reference. Of course, these new capabilities come at the cost of training, technology, and time required to fully understand the available tools. Chapter 7 assesses the potential payoff, risks, and costs associated with an XBRL initiative in more detail.

Change in the field of financial reporting is inevitable, owing to the advent of the web and related advances in IT, including XBRL-based reporting. From the perspective of the evolution of accounting profes-

sional and accounting firms, ignoring web-related technologies would
be like accountants of the late 1980s refusing to give up paper journals
in favor of electronic spreadsheets. Exhibit 2.4 lists a sample of the major
opportunities for the accounting industry that have surfaced as a direct
result of XBRL-based reporting.

XBRL-based reporting represents a new source of revenue generation for technology-savvy accounting professionals. For example,
advanced yet affordable custom financial reporting that suits the client's
unique requirements opens the door to high-level, strategy-based consulting services that complement traditional reporting-related consultation. Although custom reporting is possible with traditional reporting
systems, creating these reports is typically time consuming and highly
resource intensive. Not only must an accountant familiar with the
client's needs be involved in defining the report, but the actual report
creation typically requires the assistance of a programmer. With the
appropriate software utility, creating a custom XBRL report can be
made as simple as creating a word processing document. Given minimal
guidance from an accountant, an assistant could easily create the desired
custom report templates that would satisfy the client's needs.

EXHIBIT 2.4

OPPORTUNITIES FOR ACCOUNTING
Bundling with other services
Conversion services
Custom reporting services
Data hosting services
Education of business professionals
Expanded geographical territory
High-level consultation
Investment services
More frequent customer interaction
New markets
Real-time client support

Offering high-level consultation services has the potential to increase the quality and frequency of customer interactions, and increased value to clients translates to increased revenue for accountants. Instead of interacting with clients on a quarterly or annual basis, clients can access their reporting data and discuss their analysis with accounting professionals anytime and anywhere, thanks to wireless Web technology. Just as a cell phone or wireless PDA can be used to check the status of a publicly traded stock, Web-enabling financial data through XBRL enables corporate executives of private or unlisted companies to monitor the financial health of their companies on a minute-by-minute basis. The same technology greatly expands the geographical territory that an accounting firm or individual accountant can service.

The conversion process from paper-based reporting or non–XBRL-based reporting to an XBRL-based system represents opportunities for conversion services, education, and hosting. Conversion may require a one-time rekeying of data or, preferably, the use of conversion utilities made by third parties. Accounting firms also can be involved in the education of corporate accountants and senior management, offering training on how to take advantage of XBRL technology. Web hosting involves providing the server space and Web tools for a client's XBRL data so that they can be accessed by reporting agencies with the appropriate access privileges. An accounting firm with a modest technical staff could provide this IT-related service. Bundling accounting services with IT and related services opens up new markets, especially with the management of smaller companies that don't have the resources or desire to invest in a modest IT infrastructure. Accounting firms similarly can partner with financial planning professionals to offer clients a complete portfolio of investment services.

The potential revenue for the accounting firms that integrate XBRL reporting data and a modest IT infrastructure is limited only by the entrepreneurial spirit of accountants. It's clear that the successful accounting firm of the near future will employ not only accountants with advanced training but also professional partners with experience in analysis and IT, so that it can provide clients with a host of new value-added services, such as up-to-date analyses of their companies' performance.

Business Models

In considering the opportunities afforded by a more effective financial reporting system, it's important to recognize that financial reporting is only one of several back-end operations essential for the life of a corporation. Most corporate resources are necessarily focused on revenue-generating areas, such as sales, marketing, orders, order processing, shipping, and production planning, as opposed to back-end processes, such as financial reporting, payroll, computer services, janitorial services, or insurance. Furthermore, for corporate management, except for the internal reports that can aid in decision making and production, most of the financial reporting process is viewed as an unavoidable cost of doing business. This view is especially prevalent in regard to the cost and time that must be expended to comply with guidelines for federal and state reporting.

Timely, accurate financial reporting data is invaluable to management and to corporate decision making, regardless of the underlying business model. However, the attractiveness of moving to an XBRL-based reporting system is a function of the corporate business model, in that some models have more potential synergy with XBRL-based reporting than others. For example, in a centralized business model with strong, centralized leadership and tight control over the core competency and back-end processes (see Exhibit 2.5), there is already a high-bandwidth connection between management and the back-end processes. As a result, sharing financial reporting data in a web-compatible form is less valuable to management for internal decision-making

EXHIBIT 2.5

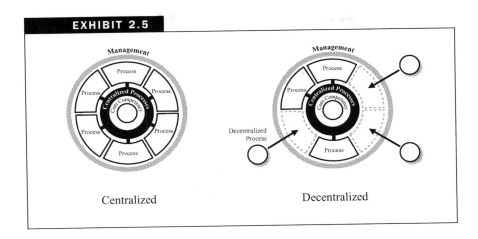

Centralized   Decentralized

purposes than it is in a business operated according to a decentralized business model.

A business operated according to a decentralized model is more likely to involve back-end processes that require less direct oversight and that are more often geographically disparate. In the decentralized business model, there is no central locus of information control, and the local department or company division typically handles its own financial reporting. Reports are forwarded to the central management on a monthly or quarterly basis, but most of the decision making is local to the process. The decentralized model provides flexibility at the cost of poor integration of business processes and redundancy throughout the organization. With less direct management of these decentralized units, regardless of whether the units are free-standing corporate entities around the globe or departments distributed within a sprawling campus, the instantaneous data access that web-enabled XBRL-based reporting provides is highly desirable as an aid to corporate decision making.

A corporation in which the financial reporting function is completely outsourced (see Exhibit 2.6) can benefit considerably from XBRL-based financial reporting. Even modest geographical separation of corporate management from the outside vendor can result in a loss

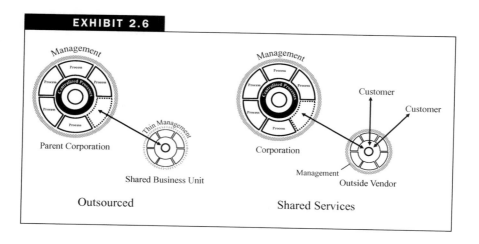

EXHIBIT 2.6

Management
Process
Centralized Process
Process

Parent Corporation

Thin Management

Shared Business Unit

Outsourced

Management
Process
Centralized Process
Process

Corporation

Management

Customer

Customer

Outside Vendor

Shared Services

of control and subsequent delays in data required for decision making. Loss of control is especially problematic when backend business functions are delegated to an outside vendor who serves a number of other clients.

Outsourcing is usually done to save costs, including avoiding hiring full-time employees for short-term projects. It is done when the job requires a high skill level but its product has little demand. A one-time retooling of a manufacturing business or conversion of an existing computer system to a new system is an example. A potential downside of outsourcing is a relative lack of control over the accounting firm's services.

A corporation configured according to a shared services business model, in which accounting services are moved to an external business unit and the parent corporation remains the main or sole customer (see Exhibit 2.6), also can benefit from XBRL-based reporting. Initially the parent corporation is the sole client of the shared business unit. Eventually the unit evolves into a for-profit outside service with multiple customers. The advantages of XBRL-based reporting become evident later in the life of the shared business unit, when it may have no ties to the parent corporation. At that point, financial reporting and other accounting services can be considered outsourced functions, with an even greater need for a real-time reporting link between accounting and the upper level management of the larger corporation.

In addition to these core business models, numerous alternative models have synergies with Web-enabled reporting using XBRL. Examples of these models include insourcing, which is a strategy in which underused internal resources are redirected, and cosourcing, a combination of insourcing and outsourcing in which a third party provides resources as an extension of the company's resources. Regardless of the model, the more decentralized and geographically disparate the accounting service from corporate management, the more important is Web access to financial data that can assist management in decision making.

Size Matters

Moving immediately to an XBRL-based system of reporting may not be as compelling for large corporations that face multiple constraints on modernizing legacy systems as it is for small companies and small accounting firms. Just as Conglomerate, Inc. in the scenario used a proprietary EDI system and required its suppliers to do the same, larger firms may have enough influence to establish their own standards with which small firms must comply. For example, a bank that services a Fortune 500 company may be happy to rekey the company's general ledger and other reporting data into its computer system in order to keep the senior management of the company happy.

In addition, as the head of IT with Conglomerate noted, there are many competing standards on the web, and moving from an established EDI standard, albeit a local one, to an evolving standard, such as XBRL, is inherently risky. A multinational company with an established, workable matrix of proprietary EDI systems may have too much invested in the system to contemplate a move to XBRL. An exception to this rule is when XBRL interfaces can be established within the existing system to slowly migrate the large corporation toward an XBRL-compliant system. Chapter 6 considers migrating to XBRL reporting from an existing digital reporting system in more detail.

Alternatives

The opportunities associated with XBRL are many. However, the concept of a standard vocabulary for business transactions and for financial reporting isn't new, nor is XBRL without competition. XBRL's main impediments to universal adoption by business are associated with legacy EDI systems and other XML-based languages, such as ebXML (extended business XML).

Electronic data interchange (EDI) is an entrenched technology throughout the world for business transactions. Large corporations that can afford to invest in EDI systems have traditionally realized significant savings over doing business with paper invoices, receipts, and related tracking documents. EDI systems differ from XML-based systems primarily in their difficulty to learn and the time involved in editing and modifying forms and reports. Making changes in an EDI system typically requires programmers familiar with BASIC, COBOL, or some other compiled programming language. Furthermore, since every EDI system is different, every programming task involves new challenges and uncertainties that result in an extended development and maintenance cycle.

There's also the inertia of EDI systems owing to their massive size. It isn't uncommon for a corporation to have 1,000 or more suppliers linked by a proprietary EDI system. Since a node on an EDI network can easily run $1,000 or more plus monthly maintenance, most small suppliers are interested in recouping their initial investment before embarking on an upgrade scheme that involves XBRL or any other evolving standard.

As noted in the scenario with Conglomerate, Inc., the primary issue with EDI is that the investment companies have an extensive, expensive

EDI infrastructure. Modifying this infrastructure to accommodate XBRL-based reporting represents added complexity and potential interference with the EDI system. Adding access to the Internet increases demands on finite corporate IT resources that must be directed toward the maintenance of an Internet-based communications system. For example, compared to a closed, private network, the Internet presents a variety of challenges, from security to ensuring that personnel don't abuse the network's limited bandwidth by downloading audio and video files for entertainment.

In many cases, the attractiveness of the Internet as a communications medium varies as a function of the availability of high-speed connectivity. In many areas of the United States and the world, 56K dialup connectivity is the best that's readily available and affordable. In contrast, most EDI systems use dedicated networks for secure, dedicated connections for the transport of corporate data to and from corporate headquarters and the suppliers in the EDI network.

Even with the advantages of stability and an installed base, many EDI systems lack key features that XBRL-based reporting promises to provide (see Exhibit 2.7). From a financial reporting perspective, EDI systems are limited because they're primarily transaction based and not designed to track historical financial data. In addition, the extensibility of a typical EDI system is low, because they are built with conventional programming languages and tools. Instead of simply adding new tags with a simple utility to define new variables, programmers must modify complex interfaces one by one. Most EDI systems rely on custom interfaces that are unique to the two systems involved and based on a proprietary communications protocol. This is because companies typically have an internal computer system and management isn't willing to simply replace a multimillion-dollar system with one that happens to be compatible with a specific EDI solution. Furthermore, EDI is based on transaction sets that define the fields, the order of these fields, and the

EXHIBIT 2.7

Feature	XBRL	ebXML	Traditional EDI
Extensibility	High	High	Low
Penetration	Low	Low	Low
Network	Internet	Internet	VAN
Security	Moderate	Moderate	High
Cost/Installation	Low	Low	High
Geographical extent	Unlimited	Unlimited	Unlimited
Web compatible	Yes	Yes	No
Open system	Yes	Yes	No
Infrastructure	XML	XML	C/BASIC/COBOL
Stability	Evolving	Evolving	Stable
Flexibility	High	High	Low
Interfaces	Single	Single	Multiple
Business rules	Separate	Separate	Embedded
Standards	Industry	Industry	Corporation
Transaction sets	Variable	Variable	Fixed
Standards evolution	Moderate	Moderate	Slow
Fixed costs	Low	Low	High

length of fields in a transaction. As a result, a company may have several separate and incompatible EDI systems, one for each company with which it does business, as illustrated in Exhibit 2.8. In this example, a seller has multiple buyers, each requiring a separate EDI network connection. Moreover, each connection typically requires a separate EDI interface and network.

Since most traditional EDI systems don't use the Internet as a communications medium, they tend to be more secure than systems based on XBRL or any other Internet-based language. In addition, EDI systems tend to have elaborate security provisions, including encryption of all data on the network. EDI is commonly implemented on proprietary value-added networks (VANs). The added value these networks provide include data validation and conversion, logging for audit trails, accountability, and transaction rollback to support uncommitted transactions.

Another challenge XBRL faces is from the many variations of XML that are being applied to business transactions and financial and business reporting. As mentioned, XML is inherently extensible. Adding a tag to define a new data type requires only a few keystrokes. This has led to an

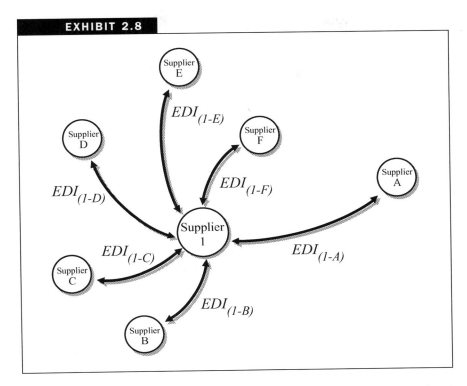

EXHIBIT 2.8

abundance of XML–based alternatives to XBRL. In addition to local vocabularies developed to address the specific needs of departments or companies, variants of XML are backed by national and international standards committees. ebXML is perhaps the foremost XML variant in the business area.

ebXML is positioned more as a replacement for traditional EDI than as a specific alternative to XBRL-based reporting. Like other XML derivatives, ebXML was born around 2000, soon after XML was introduced to the Internet community. The two organizations that are credited with establishing the standard vocabulary now known as ebXML are the Organization for the Advancement of Structured Information Standards (OASIS) and the United Nations Centre for Trade Facilitation and Electronic Business (UN/CEFACT). However, it's important to note that, just as XBRL is a set of specifications for a language, ebXML isn't a software package or service but a language that can be used to create software products.

Multiple XML standards create a conundrum for some IT department heads who want to migrate proprietary EDI systems to open, Internet-enabled systems. As listed in Exhibit 2.7, ebXML shares many of the characteristics of XBRL by virtue of the common XML parent. One of the major issues with both standards is security; any system on the Internet is susceptible to attacks by viruses and focused attacks by hackers. This weakness exists in spite of Internet services that provide for security, accountability, remote messaging, and more. The global issue with ebXML, XBRL, and other business communications languages and technologies that rely on the Internet as a communications conduit is creating a critical mass of users. As discussed in more detail in Chapter 3, standards are valuable only to the degree that there is a significant user base behind them.

Summary

The prospect of universal XBRL-based reporting represents major opportunities for the accounting industry and the corporations that it serves. The attraction of an XBRL-based reporting system is a function of the company's size, underlying business model, legacy systems, and competing technologies. The many opportunities associated with XBRL aren't free, however. Accounting professionals will have to prepare themselves for a role that's increasingly a high-level consultancy instead of forms-directed, fee-for-service work. Soon the typical accounting practice will have to employ one or more technology specialists and be prepared to offer services such as Web hosting to provide value-added services to its clients. Although change in the accounting industry is inevitable, especially the eventual movement to Internet-based reporting services, it isn't clear whether XBRL will be the change agent. Competing XML-based languages, such as ebXML, may either coexist with XBRL or compete with it for financial reporting.

A little knowledge that acts is worth more than much knowledge that is idle.

—**Kahlil Gibran,** *The Prophet*

CHAPTER 3

Standards

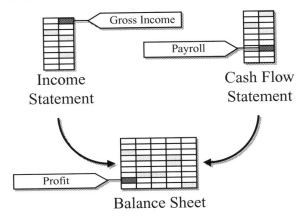

After reading this chapter you will be able to

- Understand how standards, not technology per se, are necessary to move the financial reporting industry forward

- Understand the significance of standards organizations in initiating change in the finance industry

- Appreciate the role of information technology vendors and developers in shaping reporting standards

- Understand how the evolution of standards in the general computer industry affects financial reporting standards

- Appreciate the role of government in facilitating and forcing the move toward reporting standards

In information-intensive industries, automation through computerization and other forms of information technology (IT) is often promoted as the means to increased productivity and efficiency. In theory, automating any information-based operation in a way that leverages data will contribute to the bottom line. In reality, IT may be necessary, but it's never sufficient in itself to ensure increased efficiency and profitability.

For example, consider the value of a single telephone, fax machine, or computer with a Web browser but no connection to the Internet. These and other technologies are valuable only to the extent that there are other users of the same technology using the same language on the same network infrastructure. In computer science circles, this observation is commonly referred to as Metcalf's Law, coined by Bob Metcalf, inventor of the Ethernet and a venture capitalist. His law states that the value of a network is proportional to the number of users of the network squared. An assumption of the law is that the users are adhering to a common, standard means of communicating. That is, standards enable information technologies to be used to increase corporate efficiency and profitability. High standards are also what makes accounting a professional activity that requires considerable education and experience.

The chapter explores XBRL-enabled reporting from the perspective of standards—in terms of practices and organizations. It begins with an examination of the traditions—a form of standards—of the finance industry. It also considers the effect of online transactions and the roles in shaping modern reporting standards played by vendors, governments, international trade organizations, and the general computing industry.

Rules of the Game

In most of the world, making—and keeping—money is regulated by a host of rules or standards. Illegal activities generally involve generating capital without the permission of the local or national government and without the requisite monitoring of activity and associated taxation. Of the recognized forms of legal capital-generating processes, the one responsible for the majority of the wealth generated worldwide is

Sarbanes–Oxley Act of 2002

One of the most far-reaching changes to reporting standards for public corporations resulted from passage of the Sarbanes-Oxley Act (SOA) in July 2002. The contents of the Act reflect the public pressure on the government to prevent the repeat of an Enron event. The SOA, which includes 1,107 sections, enacts standards in these areas:

- Public Company Oversight Boards
- Auditor Independence
- Corporate Responsibility
- Enhanced Financial Disclosures
- Analyst Conflicts of Interest
- Commission Resources and Authority
- Studies and Reports
- Corporate and Criminal Fraud Accountability
- White-Collar Crime Penalty Enhancements
- Corporate Tax Returns
- Corporate Fraud and Accountability

Of particular note is Section 108 of the SOA, Accounting Standards, which:

> ". . . considers, in adopting accounting principles, the need to keep standards current in order to reflect changes in the business environment, the extent to which international convergence in high quality accounting standards is necessary or appropriate in the public interest and for the protection of investors."

The SOA doesn't change the GAAP. However, it does authorize the SEC to recognize as "generally accepted" any accounting principles established by a standard-setting body organized in

IN THE REAL WORLD CONTINUED

accordance with the Act. In addition, even if an issuer's financial statements comply with GAAP, they could violate the requirements of "fair presentation," thereby imposing criminal liability on the corporation's chief executive and chief financial officers.

embodied in the form of a corporation. However, simply having a corporation doesn't guarantee compliance with standards, and, as the infamous Enron debacle illustrates, in some cases what is considered standard practice is interpreted rather fancifully.

As legal entities, corporations date back to the Middle Ages, when they were used to organize monasteries, guilds, and universities. They became a major method of capital generation and of sharing risk for voyages of exploration and discovery in the 16th century. In the United States, corporations, which are governed by states, began in 1811, when New York established the laws defining the procedure for becoming a corporation. As a capital-generating engine, the corporation came into its own during the Industrial Revolution, when large amounts of capital investment were required to sustain the growth of factories.

Taxation in the United States became a federal institution in 1862 with the formation of the Internal Revenue Service (IRS), which was given the responsibility of "encouraging voluntary compliance" with the tax laws and regulations. As part of the tax assessment process, corporations were required to report gross profits—interest income, dividend income, capital gain, rents, and royalties—balanced against costs of production—salaries, wages, and benefits to employees, compensation to corporate officers, advertising, and facilities maintenance. Collecting all of these data in a timely, orderly fashion required the institution of standard accounting practices so that the books could be kept, ready for inspection by IRS representatives.

With the concentration of large amounts of capital in the hands of a few—sometimes less than honest—individuals, fraud became rampant. To protect the unwary citizens of the early 20th century from fraudulent get-rich-quick schemes, the Securities and Exchange Commission (SEC) was created in the early 1930s. The SEC established the rules of fair play regarding the national securities exchanges, and it was empowered to monitor the activity of corporations, primarily through mandatory reporting.

Since the early 20th century, the reporting requirements of corporations and other recognized forms of doing business have increased in complexity to the point that typically highly trained professionals are hired to compile and format the data required by federal, state, and local government agencies. Paradoxically, one of the major technological innovations of the 20th century, the computer, hasn't simplified the accounting process. Instead, since the introduction of the PC and electronic spreadsheet in the mid-1980s, the widespread computerization of the accounting practice has had the indirect effect of *increasing* the complexity and volume of reporting. As the new computer-based methods became standard practice, they diffused into the accounting community, and old paper-based practices were discarded. As a result, PCs are no longer optional accessories; they're an essential component of the accountant's toolkit. Because government agencies that required reporting viewed the computerized accounting industry as more capable than the paper-based one, new, more comprehensive reporting requirements were instituted.

The digital corporation and virtually universal access to the Internet enables reporting that is comprehensive and timely, so reporting requirements are likely to keep growing. Since IT permeates the modern business environment, corporate management can't claim that abiding by reporting standards represents an unreasonable burden. Modern data-gathering and processing technology is standard fare in virtually every business, from the corner grocery store to a Fortune 500 company.

EDGAR Analyst LLC

EDGAR Online, Inc., and Universal Business Matrix LLC formed a joint venture, EDGAR Analyst LLC, to provide the first global XBRL data exchange. EDGAR Online, Inc., already provides access to global company information from over 13,000 companies in 45 countries on a pay-per-view basis. What makes this venture notable is that EDGAR Analyst LLC will provide public financial data in XBRL format, along with a set of XBRL-enabled analytic and conversion tools.

The initial focus is on annual and quarterly financial reports on U.S. public companies; the aim eventually is to include *all* public companies globally. In addition to a suite of analytic tools, the company is developing software tools that companies can use to automate the conversion of financial data to XBRL for inclusion in the global data exchange and for submission to regulatory agencies.

What makes a central, XBRL-format repository of all public business financials so compelling is that it can be mined for relationships in data that may not be obvious to a human observer. Data mining the financials of over 13,000 companies is likely to discover financial indicators of trends in the U.S. and world economies that haven't been discovered through conventional analysis.

Issues

The continued evolution of the rules for creating and retaining wealth and the associated genesis of the professional accountant highlights several key issues:

- Standards organizations and technology vendors play a critical role in establishing reporting standards by providing the means of diffusing technology and knowledge of how to use it throughout the industry.

- Government plays a major role in establishing and enforcing reporting standards.

- Technological advances have redefined what is considered acceptable accounting practice, especially in terms of complexity and timeliness of reporting.

- Reporting requirements will continue to evolve, paralleling the availability of affordable information technologies and changes in the political landscape.

The following section expands on these and related issues.

Evolution of Standards

Accounting standards typically evolve over years and decades, in part because of the inertia of the financial system, including general conservatism and resistance to change, and because compromises generally must be resolved between the major stakeholders involved in any major change. For example, in response to scandals at Enron Corp., WorldCom Inc., and Arthur Andersen LLP, the U.S. Congress passed the Sarbanes-Oxley Act of 2002 (SOA). One effect of the Act was the creation of the Public Company Accounting Oversight Board in July 2002 to police auditors. Prior to that time, the SEC was largely self-regulated.

In addition to the technology-driven changes discussed earlier, there are political forces behind changes in reporting standards. For example, for the 30 years prior to passage of the SOA, the deadlines for filing public company quarterly and annual reports were 45 and 90 days after the end of the quarter, respectively. However, in response to financial disclosure and reporting issues highlighted by the collapse of Enron Corporation, the SEC shortened the deadline for filing public company quarterly and annual reports to 30 and 60 days, respectively. Although this new requirement doesn't directly dictate electronic reporting, complying with the shorter reporting time is much less burdensome for companies filing electronically with the SEC than for companies preparing and mailing the paper forms.

Establishing new standards of any type typically isn't easy, and this is especially true in the conservative financial accounting industry. For example, because large corporations and accounting firms can't be expected to change fundamental reporting processes overnight, the SOA specifies changes to filing deadlines that are phased in over three years, with no change for the first year. The annual report deadline was set to 90 days for the first year, 75 days for the second year, and 60 days for the third year and thereafter. The quarterly report deadline was established at 45 days for the first year, 40 days for the second year, and 35 days for the third year.

In addition to the inertia inherent in every sizable bureaucracy, there are often active opponents to change because it either upsets their method of doing business or otherwise costs them time and money. For example, several large German firms, including DaimlerChrysler AG and Siemens AG, petitioned the SEC for an exemption to the Sarbanes-Oxley Act, on the grounds that complying with the new stock exchange standards was overly burdensome, in part because the SOA conflicts with the corporate governance structure used by German corporations.

Stakeholders

The stakeholder analysis in Exhibit 3.1 depicts the major stakeholders affected by a move to XBRL-based reporting standards. Some of the stakeholders more adversely affected by the move from paper or proprietary reporting systems to electronic systems include the suppliers of paper forms and software developers of non–XBRL-compatible reporting systems. Other stakeholders negatively affected include corporate IT departments burdened by the need to establish and maintain the electronic infrastructure and those professional accountants and smaller

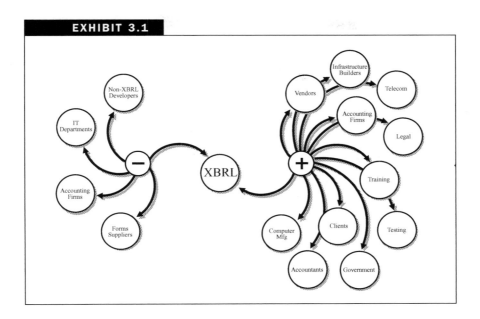

EXHIBIT 3.1

accounting firms unwilling or unable to make the change to the new reporting paradigm. If the industry moves to paperless reporting, the downside to paper forms suppliers and the companies that write the software that produces traditional printed reports is obvious. Corporate IT departments may be challenged initially to provide the infrastructure and support for an XBRL-based system of reporting that relies on the Internet and Web browsers for the communications infrastructure. This challenge may be especially evident in a corporation that has a policy against allowing Internet access through its closed internal network or intranet. Opening up a closed network to the Internet brings security concerns and potential employee abuses of the system that will require IT resources to resolve the issues.

Smaller accounting firms and individual accountants who aren't versed in electronic reporting or IT in general also may be negatively affected by the switch to XBRL-based reporting. Although XBRL eventually will be integrated transparently into every major accounting package, accountants who deal primarily with small business and corporate clients will have to adapt their practice to fit the new realities of electronic reporting. Successful accountants will develop the flexibility to shift into more of a consulting role and to offer the array of services that their competition will certainly offer.

In contrast to the short list of negative stakeholders, the list of stakeholders who can benefit from a switch to XBRL-based reporting standards is extensive. It includes various technology vendors and manufacturers (e.g., accounting software vendors, computer manufacturers, and telecommunications infrastructure builders), the government, and service organizations that are poised to offer accountants training and testing. It also includes accounting firms and accountants, the legal industry, and accounting firms' clients. The degree to which technology vendors will benefit from the move to XBRL-based reporting is a function of the technical status of specific accounting firms. Those accounting firms that are fully computerized and that provide their staff with unrestricted access to the Internet may need relatively little in terms of additional hardware and software, other than the XBRL-compatible reporting packages. However, even firms with open Internet access may require additional hardware to enhance both the performance of the XBRL language and the level of security. For example, even though it may seem unnecessary to secure a system designed to post corporate quarterly and annual reports openly and freely on the Internet, lack of security can be detrimental to the company if a hacker falsifies the reports to indicate higher or lower corporate earnings.

Accounting firms without a high-speed Internet connection and little or no internal experience with servers and databases represent a newfound market for technology vendors and IT consultants. The widespread adoption of XBRL-based reporting and the resulting transformation of the accounting industry into a technology-savvy consultancy are predicated on having an information infrastructure capable of providing custom report generation, archiving, and Web hosting services. It also requires accountants who are fluent in a variety of XBRL-enabled analysis software tools that are appearing on the market.

As XBRL is adopted by the accounting industry, a window of opportunity has opened for training, testing, and certification centers and organizations. Every practicing business accountant will have to be able to create custom reports and to understand their relevance to the client's ability to stay competitive. Eventually the shift in focus will be reflected in the certification requirements for accountants as well as in a new training curriculum for them. Other groups that stand to be positively affected by XBRL include the legal industry, in part because it will be easier to police the accounting industry, given the ready access to public accounting data. Finally, the government stands to gain from the increased speed of reporting. It's highly likely that in the near future, government reporting agencies will either no longer accept paper reports or charge extra to process paper reports.

Standards Adoption

Standards adoption generally entails more than a decree from a governing body or board dictating the use of one technology or process over another. Rather, standards evolve over time, and they lag behind the availability of a new technology because the technology must be proven before it can be endorsed by a standards organization. One way to understand the interaction of the availability of a new technology, such as XBRL, and the acceptance of the technology as a standard is to use the Co-Evolution Model shown in Exhibit 3.2. This model suggests that an important factor affecting the establishment of a new standard is the coevolution of technology, standards, and users of the technology. Old standards are transformed into new standards as old technologies are replaced by new technologies.

In the Co-Evolution Model, old technologies, such as paper-based financial reporting systems, are gradually replaced by new technologies

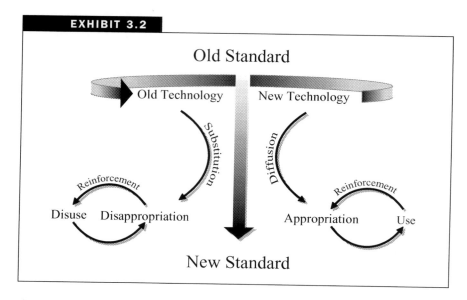

EXHIBIT 3.2

Old Standard

Old Technology   New Technology

Substitution   Diffusion

Reinforcement   Reinforcement

Disuse   Disappropriation   Appropriation   Use

New Standard

through the processes of substitution and diffusion. Substitution occurs when a new technology is substituted for an older technology, such as when electronic financial reporting is substituted for paper-based reporting. Diffusion describes the adoption or appropriation of a new technology. Diffusion is a function of the rate of appropriation of the technology, which is in turn a function of the positive reinforcement that users receive when they work with the technology. The model highlights the three-way interaction among standards, technologies, and the users of the technology.

The appropriation of a new technology is facilitated by positive personal, peer, and functional reinforcement. For example, if an accountant in a firm using an XBRL-compatible accounting system gets her work done faster than before, the new, high-speed system becomes part of her identity, to the same extent that a sports car defines its driver. She's also likely to invest time and energy into learning the new accounting system and modifying it to suit her preferences and needs. That is, she appropriates the technology and is transformed in the process. Her expectations of what a reporting system can deliver in terms of speed and comprehensiveness have been permanently altered by her experience with the new technology.

The Co-Evolution Model also highlights how a new technology eventually becomes old technology when a faster, easier-to-use, or more feature-laden technology becomes available. As a result, all technologies and associated standards must be eventually replaced. For example, consider the case of the videotape player. A multibillion-dollar video rental market suggests that the concept of the videotape player and the rental of prerecorded tapes is a valid business proposition. However, the first videotape standard to market, the now-discontinued Sony BetaMax, while technically superior to JVC's competing Video Home System (VHS) standard, succumbed to the simpler and more popular VHS standard in the home market. Similarly, DVD technology, with its superior image and sound quality, is poised to devour the VHS market.

In the model, the technology modifies the user as she interacts with it, and this enables a new standard to be established. What's more, not only is this cycle continually progressing, but the pace of technological innovation accelerates. As such, the process of appropriation and then disappropriation of new technology is speeding up. In addition, the substitution and diffusion are a function of government legislation, vendors, and standards organizations. For example, the old technology standard is no longer the paper general ledger but the stand-alone PC and accounting package that replaced it. The new technology standard is the Internet, along with the wired and wireless Web, and extensible languages such as XBRL.

Communications Standards

XBRL is a communications facilitator. An appreciation for XBRL's relationship to communications theory is important in understanding the significance of the technology in electronic financial reporting. In addition, the language of paper-based financial reporting and the underlying characteristics of XBRL are all relevant to enabling the electronic communications of financial reporting data.

Communications Theory

Classic communications theory, developed by Claude Shannon in the 1940s, offers a model that can be used to describe virtually any communications system, including financial reporting. This model is shown graphically in Exhibit 3.3.

According to Shannon's model, the major components are a data source, a transmitter, a medium, a noise source, a receiver, and a data destination. The data source generates a message that is sent to a transmitter, which generates a signal that propagates through a medium such as a cable or the ether. In its course from transmitter to receiver, the signal is influenced by a noise source—interference from other signals in the cable, for example. Once at the receiver, the signal is decoded, and the resulting message is sent to the destination. This model offers an abstract view of communications that can be easily adapted to illustrate the benefits of XBRL.

EXHIBIT 3.3

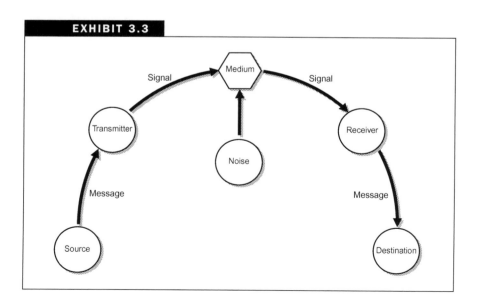

Mapping the traditional business reporting process to the communications model illustrates some of the limitations of the pre-XBRL approach. As shown in Exhibit 3.4, reporting data commonly reside in electronic form in an accounting application, either in the corporation's accounting department or in an external accounting firm. Because there are no direct, transparent communications between the accounting application and the application at, for example, the Internal Revenue Service (IRS), the report must be rekeyed by a typist. As shown in the exhibit, data from the accounting package are transformed into a paper report, which is transmitted to the IRS or other government agency where the data are rekeyed by the typist.

The typist is the medium through which the signal must pass on its way to the report database in the agency. However, this medium isn't error free; errors due to mistyping are introduced in the transfer of data from printed to digital form. While it's possible to use an optical character recognition (OCR) device to scan the paper report automatically,

EXHIBIT 3.4

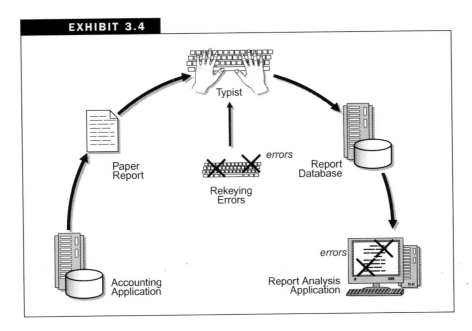

obviating the need for manual rekeying of the report, even the best OCR systems have an error rate of about 1 percent, or about 1 erroneous character or digit out of every 100.

Regardless of how the data are transferred from printed to digital form, eventually they are routed to a report database, where they can be reviewed with a report analysis application. Because the errors introduced by the typist appear in the final analysis, the rekeyed data may need to be compared with the paper report—an expensive and time-consuming proposition.

Exhibit 3.5 illustrates the communications of financial reporting data to the appropriate reporting agency using XBRL. An accounting application formats the data into an electronic XBRL document in which data elements are tagged. This electronic document is then sent through the Internet—a journey that may involve thousands of kilometers of cable and hundreds of routers, bridges, firewalls, and other hardware devices—to the reporting agency's internal network or

EXHIBIT 3.5

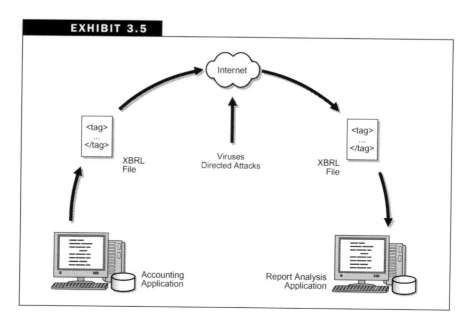

intranet and finally to the report analysis application. Although the complexity of the Internet is hidden in this illustration, it includes numerous checks and security measures to help ensure errorless transmission of signals from one location or node to another. Even so, the Internet isn't necessarily an error-free medium. Errors can occur due to equipment failure or attack from hackers and viruses. However, assuming proper security precautions are in place, the XBRL file that appears in the report analysis application should be an error-free copy of the original document.

It's also important to note here that the electronic communications model illustrated in Exhibit 3.5 isn't limited to XBRL-based reporting. It can be applied to virtually any system involving the electronic submission of financial reporting data. As long as the transmitter and receiver abide by the same standard and the medium is relatively free of noise, the signal should remain intact. Furthermore, as long as the message formats agree—for example, they're based on XBRL—then the meaning of the data can be communicated as well.

In this regard, it's important to distinguish the message from the signal, which is made explicit in Exhibit 3.3. The communications hardware and software, from the workstation operating system to the myriad devices and software systems that constitute the local intranet and the global Internet, are based on standards that allow the message to be communicated from one point to another. However, it is the agreement on a message format—in this example, XBRL—that allows an electronic document to be interpreted seamlessly by the recipient. For example, it does the accounting firm little good if its accounting application generates a financial report in a proprietary format that can't be interpreted or opened by the reporting agency's analysis application. As a parallel, the reason that most text documents exchanged on the Internet are in Microsoft Word format is because it's the most common text document format in corporate America. Virtually everyone in the business world has an application on the PC that can open a document that is in Microsoft Word format, even if they're using WordPerfect or some other document editor.

Financial Reporting

Financial and business reporting is a form of communications in itself. What distinguishes traditional reporting from a simple string of data is that the format of the data is often as important as the data themselves. For example, consider the Income Statement, the report of revenues and expenses over an accounting period. Since net income—the difference between revenues and expenses—usually appears at the bottom of the statement, the income amount is often referred to as the bottom line. This reference to the bottom line is common, even if the income figure appears at the top of a spreadsheet. However, most accountants expect to see the bottom line or income figure at the bottom of an income report.

Similarly, the balance sheet has a standard format that is readily recognized by all accountants and reporting agencies. As shown in Exhibit 3.6, the balance sheet is divided into three sections, Assets, Liabilities, and Equity. This layout facilitates human interpretation of the fundamental accounting equation:

$$ASSETS = LIABILITIES + EQUITY$$

Because electronic spreadsheets typically are used to create linear documents, the balance sheet often appears as a single column of data. However, the integrity of the three sections is maintained, as in the balance sheet shown in Exhibit 3.7.

Furthermore, within each of the three sections of the balance sheet, the layout of the data is standardized. For example, to record an increase in cash, an entry is made on the left-hand, or debit, side of the Cash account. Conversely, a decrease in cash is recorded on the right-hand, or

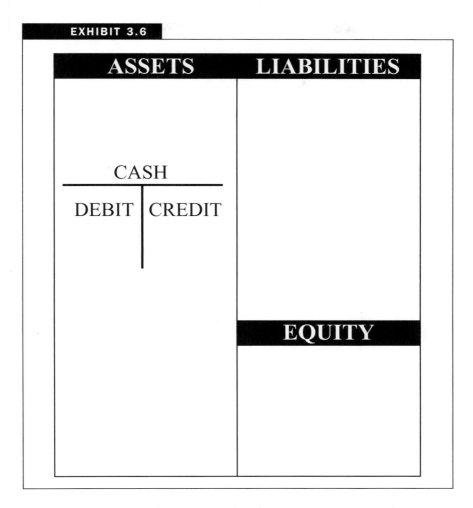

EXHIBIT 3.6

ASSETS | LIABILITIES

CASH

DEBIT | CREDIT

EQUITY

credit, side of the Cash account. This format convention makes it easy for an accountant to verify that the data support another basic accounting equation:

$$DEBITS = CREDITS$$

When listed in a report, the customary format is to list the debit first, in a left-hand column, and the credit second, in the right-hand column. This format is standard in computer-generated reports as well as in traditional paper forms-based accounting.

EXHIBIT 3.7

BALANCE SHEET

ASSETS
Cash	4,000	
Equipment	2,000	
Furniture	5,000	
Total Assets		11,000

LIABILITIES
Accounts Payable	1,000	
Total Liabilities		1,000

EQUITY
Paid-in Capital	10,000	
Total Equity		10,000
Total Liability and Equity		11,000

Returning to Shannon's communications model, these formatting conventions can be considered part of the standard that allow the message to be more readily understood at the destination. One way to maintain a standard format is to establish a standard message format based on the position of data in the message. For example, the part of the message containing the balance sheet shown in Exhibit 3.7 could be communicated as:

4,000:

2,000:

5,000:

11,000:

1,000:

1,000:

10,000:

10,000:

11,000

As long as the recipient of the message knows that the fourth element in the string (11,000) represents total assets, there is no problem. However, if an additional asset is added to the balance sheet, the change must be communicated to the message recipient, and the mapping of position to balance sheet location must be reworked. When multiple data sources and data recipients are involved, assuring that everyone involved in sharing the data uses the new message format standard can be problematic. This is the issue with traditional EDI, which often uses a messaging scheme based on mapping the location of data in a sequence to location on a report or transaction form.

Another approach, and one facilitated by XBRL, is to tag each element in the message. Again, using the balance sheet in Exhibit 3.7 as an example of the data to be communicated, the message could take the form:

    <Assets.Cash>4,000

    <Assets.Equipment>2,000

    <Assets.Furniture>5,000

    <Assets.Total>11,000

    <Liabilities.AccountsPayable> 1,000

    <Liabilities.Total>1,000

    <Equities.PaidInCapital>10,000

    <Equities.Total>10,000

    <LiabilitiesAndEquity.Total>11,000

Note that since the data are tagged, the order isn't important. The same data could be communicated in the form:

    <LiabilitiesAndEquity.Total>11,000

    <Assets.Cash>4,000

    <Assets.Furniture>5,000

    <Liabilities.Total>1,000

<Assets.Total>11,000

<Liabilities.AccountsPayable> 1,000

<Equities.PaidInCapital>10,000

<Equities.Total>10,000

<Assets.Equipment>2,000

Because the data are tagged, their relative location can be easily manipulated at the destination, regardless of whether the data are in order or whether additional data are added to the message. The actual tag names aren't important, as long as the sender and receiver agree on a vocabulary. In addition, unlike a message that relies on strict order sequence to convey meaning, a vocabulary lexicon can be easily disseminated to the intended message recipients. Furthermore, as long as the vocabulary is sufficiently rich, data can be added to the message without the need to inform recipients of the existence of the additional data elements. For example, the value of a company car could be added to the balance sheet in Exhibit 3.7. As long as the tagging vocabulary has a tag or symbol for company car, it can be added to the message without modifying the recipient's computer system.

An additional advantage of using tagged messages in communicating reporting data is that it greatly simplifies the automatic validation of data. For example, upon the receipt of the balance sheet data, a simple test can be used to validate the data. The test can be expressed symbolically using the tags, as in:

<Assets.Total> = <Liabilities.Total> + <Equity.Total>

Note the same type of test could be performed with the colon-delimited string used as an example of an EDI message format. However, maintaining and modifying the formulas likely would require significant programming time and effort. In contrast, equations expressed symbolically remain valid, regardless of the sequence of data within the message. The issue isn't the particular vocabulary, only that it's standardized. For example, tagging works just as well when total assets are tagged as "<Total-Assets>", "<Total.Assets>", or "<Assets.Total.GeneralLedger>". What matters is that the vocabulary is standardized. Readers interested in the format of actual general ledger data tagged with XBRL are encouraged to explore the websites listed in the "Further Reading" section of this book.

Progress

In business, technology and process improvement is viewed as a means of making life easier, increasing efficacy, decreasing cost, or adding more consumer value. Similarly, the motivation behind changes in reporting technology and new standards is to improve the reporting process for accountants and their clients. Achieving progress in the financial reporting industry involves three major components: drivers, new standards, and maintenance, as displayed in Exhibit 3.8.

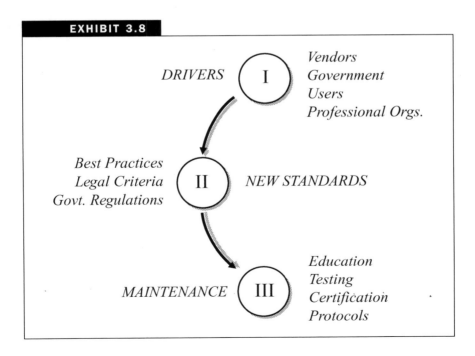

EXHIBIT 3.8

DRIVERS — I — Vendors / Government / Users / Professional Orgs.

Best Practices / Legal Criteria / Govt. Regulations — II — NEW STANDARDS

MAINTENANCE — III — Education / Testing / Certification / Protocols

The drivers for change are primarily the technology vendors, which offer information technologies that enable new reporting standards to be met efficiently and on a timely basis, often with little or no human intervention. The government is another major force for progress in the reporting arena because it stands to gain much more timely and complete reporting data and at less cost than before. Many accounting firms and some independent accountants are pushing for the adoption of XBRL-based reporting; they believe it offers the potential for value-added services and an elevation of the profession away from fee for service, and more toward high-level consulting based on the analysis of the financial reporting data. For the same reasons, professional organizations are driving XBRL adoption because it will benefit the group membership.

The next component of progress, the actual establishment of new standards, involves government regulations, such as the SOA, and industry-wide consensus that the use of XBRL reporting is consistent with best practices. The legal criteria for what constitutes best practices also must be shifted to include XBRL-based reporting. The third phase of progress in the financial reporting industry involves maintenance. Maintaining a standard requires enforcement, education, and eventual incorporation of the standard into the professional certification process. It also involves establishing and following protocols within the accounting firm that complement the established standards.

Progress doesn't stop with maintenance. Progress isn't static. It's a dynamic, constantly evolving phenomenon. As such, it's only a matter of time before an existing standard is replaced by one that's more complete, less complex, based on a newer technology, or otherwise superior for a given task. The basis for change may be a new technology, a push by vendors, politics within standards organizations, or new government regulations. For example, standards for electronic reporting would have never been established without the development of computer technology. Similarly, the Sarbanes-Oxley Act would never have been passed by the Congress had it not been for the public outcry for political action against corporate greed and mischief.

Standards shouldn't be embraced until a reasonable transition strategy is formulated. One way to make the transition is to provide for evolutionary improvement while ensuring some degree of backward compatibility. For example, Microsoft makes it easy for computer users to discard their old operating systems and replace them with a new version of Windows by providing a relatively seamless upgrade path. Many old DOS programs are compatible with the latest version of Windows when they're run within a special DOS window or shell. Similarly, programs written for the earliest version of Microsoft Windows can be run in the latest version by adjusting the operating system settings, even though there is some limitation in functionality.

XBRL and other XML-based languages appear ideally suited to evolutionary improvement because they can be extended easily to include a virtually unlimited vocabulary. Specialized XML-hardware accelerators are available to increase speed and efficiency of XBRL-based communications, which tend to be more verbose than traditional communications. Furthermore, a variety of XML software tools continue to be released on the market, underscoring the momentum in the general computing industry behind XML to accept XML and its derivatives as languages whose acceptance extends well beyond the financial community.

Of course, just as the Internet redefined business practices and made e-commerce a practical reality for companies such as Amazon.com and online stock trading companies, it's inevitable that the next new technology will further increase reporting capabilities and totally transform the standards and best practices of the accounting industry. For now, however, XBRL-based reporting appears to be uniquely positioned to provide the progress that the accounting and financial industries seek.

The next chapter examines the corporate reporting processes in detail.

Summary

In the United States, reporting practice standards have increased periodically since the formal recognition of the corporation in the 19th century. Many of today's reporting standards are the result of unscrupulous practice in the past. Most recently, the SOA was instituted to modify the initial charter of the SEC so that it is more accountable to the government. The other major drivers of reporting standards are the IT vendors, the move toward XML as a reporting and transaction language by the general computing community, and the interest of individual accountants and accounting firms in providing more and more varied value-added services to their business clients.

Few in the accounting industry would argue against a standard electronic means of publishing and maintaining financial and business data, but whether the standard should be based on XBRL, another variant of XML, or another language altogether isn't clear. What's more, whatever language is selected for the initial industry-standard electronic reporting system, eventually it will have to be replaced. This replacement language may be an evolutionary outgrowth of XBRL or a revolutionary change to something completely different.

The most successful businessman is the man who holds onto the old just as long as it is good and grabs the new just as soon as it is better.

—Robert P. Vanderpoel

CHAPTER 4

Process

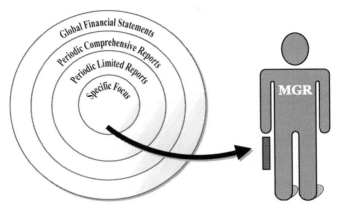

After reading this chapter you will be able to

- Appreciate the potential of XBRL beyond financial reporting
- Understand how XBRL facilitates management control
- Appreciate the role of XBRL in extending the knowledge management process outside of the corporation

F inance involves much more than completing and submitting quarterly and annual financial statements to the proper government agencies. Rather, financial reports represent the culmination of intricate and often complex processes that center on creating, capturing, transporting, and managing data—so-called knowledge management (KM). In a data-intensive field such as finance, KM principles can elevate the perception of data from a mere collection of figures to valuable intellectual property that should be treated like the lifeblood of the company. In the world of finance, there are no steel ingots or widget factories. There are only data, and the degree to which they are accurate, complete, and timely can make the difference between the success and failure of a company.

The task of managing data is facilitated by an understanding of the various ways in which data are used within and outside of the corporation. For example, the process of managing financial information is typically considered a multistage process directed by an accounting professional. Beyond fulfilling external reporting requirements, financial data can provide management with the basis for action from innovation, decision support, and process improvement, to performance assessment, and managing day-to-day operations.

The last chapter discussed how XBRL can facilitate external financial reporting, This chapter explores XBRL as an enabler of internal report-generation processes, especially reports intended for management control purposes. Topics include knowledge management principles, the role of XBRL in the financial knowledge management process, the potential of XBRL beyond financial reporting, and how a KM process built around XBRL can facilitate decision making and add to the corporate bottom line.

Through a Manager's Eyes

Management involves leadership, articulating a clear vision, making key business decisions with often incomplete or inaccurate information, and, most important, creating innovations that increase corporate competitiveness, improve the bottom line, and position the company for continued success. Understandably, many corporate managers metaphorically view themselves as generals, fighting a battle for survival of their enterprise, using corporate capital and human resources, together with their innovation, to outsmart and outmaneuver the competition and sustain or gain market share.

One reason senior managers are rewarded so highly is because they are hired with equally high expectations. Managers typically are expected

Data Overload

With the ready availability of cell phones, wireless personal digital assistants, pocket pagers, and other forms of communications tools, staying in constant touch with the workplace is often expected of corporate management. As XBRL-based operational reports become the norm and as increasingly finer levels of detail become available in wired and wireless Internet-compatible formats, it's inevitable that constant monitoring of the performance of one's department, division, or even work group will be expected, if not required. In a high-volume fast-food franchise restaurant, for example, the local manager may be expected to monitor cost of labor, which products are selling, and the cost of food—on an hourly or quarter-hour basis. The ability to monitor selected variables from an XBRL-based operational report empowers a manager to make virtually real-time decisions regarding how to best improve the business's performance. It also allows corporate management to evaluate the performance of a national or regional advertising campaign.

It's reasonable to expect chief executive managers to monitor the hour-to-hour health of their corporation's stock on one of the national exchanges. However, since the dot-com bust of 2000, there has been a significant exodus away from technology by senior managers who had been living and breathing the technology products that they thought were their ticket to riches. Without the prospect for immense gain, many of the information-savvy dot-com senior executives who landed safely in a traditional brick-and-mortar or even a click-and-mortar business eschew electronic tethers and now prefer to leave the majority of their work at the office.

However, many lower-level managers don't have a choice. Some of the same corporate senior managers who distance themselves from always-on connectivity expect their department-level managers to carry pagers in the event of emergencies while traveling and even on weekends. There may not be written rules dictating a

TIPS & TECHNIQUES CONTINUED

24 × 7 plugged-in lifestyle, but managers are made to understand that it's the road to advancement. The danger in this scenario is information overload and technology burnout.

One solution to avoiding information overload is to use the filter function that XBRL makes possible and to allow managers to monitor the top one or two performance measures, perhaps with an alarm function that alerts them of trouble.

to get a stream of profitable products or service to market in record time and to enhance them with marketing and management practices that maximize results. They must devise and properly execute business plans that provide a high return on investment for stockholders and create a strategy for keeping the competition at bay. Staying consistently ahead of the competition and innovating while avoiding dead ends isn't easy. Managers must be vigilant to keep the corporation's processes current and competitive and to surpass less innovative competitors.

Innovation is vital to survival of the organization, but its execution is risky and the cost of failure typically is high. For example, an innovative product that is technically superior to the competition may fail because its product life is limited by changes in the economy that are beyond the manager's control. Consider how many dot-coms with products and services superior to those of their competition vanished when the industry tanked.

Innovation doesn't occur in a vacuum; it requires a creative, motivated manager who has access to the appropriate business intelligence—timely, accurate data that are in a form that is easily digested and detailed enough to aid in decision making. As such, managers require data—on the business climate to respond to changing customer needs and a changing market and from inside the corporation to determine which projects deserve financial commitment and where new processes can be applied internally in an effort to increase profitability.

Managers draw on data from a variety of sources to gain a 360-degree view of their organization and the business environment, as illustrated in Exhibit 4.1. Communications with key shareholders provide managers with expectations and benchmarks that they're expected to meet or exceed. Conversations with lower-level managers provide senior managers with critical data on specific areas of the company, such as the performance of specific corporate divisions and their adherence to production schedules. Customers provide a view of the effectiveness of any ongoing customer relationship management initiatives, such as the effectiveness of the company's call centers, website, and outreach program, as well as customer satisfaction with the company's products and

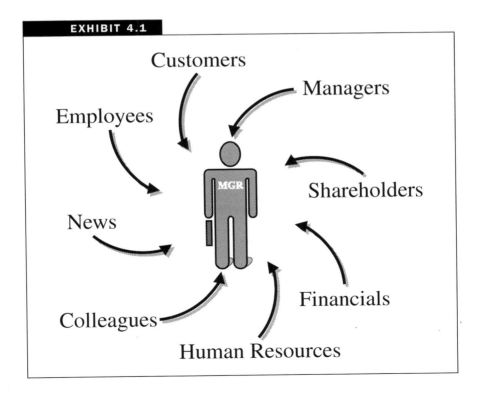

EXHIBIT 4.1

Customers

Managers

Employees

Shareholders

MGR

News

Colleagues

Financials

Human Resources

service. Data gained from employee interactions help managers monitor employee morale and job satisfaction.

The cable and print news services provide the manager with a measure of the effectiveness of any corporate public relations campaign, how the industry and economy are performing, and any external events—from war to natural disasters—that may provide opportunities for corporate expansion. Contact with colleagues in other companies and other industries provide data on the general status of business in the region. Interaction with the corporate human resources director can provide an additional measure of employee morale as well as hard numbers on employee absenteeism and other factors that may affect output volume, quality, cost, or speed.

Financials, especially internal or control reports, provide measures of corporate health in profit, cash follow, and liquidity. Of all of the measures concerning the status of the corporation, the financials must be the most accurate, quantitative business intelligence available. The perceptions of employees, colleagues, and shareholders are irrelevant if the corporate financials are in a shambles. In this regard, the management control data constitute the vital signs of the corporation. Although managers differ on how often they need to take the pulse of the corporation, when they do decide to assess the corporation's health, the financials must be available, timely, and applicable to the question at hand.

Key Concepts

The manager's reliance on data highlights several key issues:

- Managers draw on a variety of data sources, many of which provide inconclusive or incomplete data.
- Managers rely on both quantitative and qualitative measures of corporate performance.
- The business intelligence available to managers varies considerably in timeliness, quality, and quantity.

You Can't Have Everything

XBRL-based operational reporting promises to be a boon for management in the high-volume, fast-paced businesses characteristic of the modern click-and-mortar enterprise. However, regardless of the available technology, it isn't possible for a manager to have everything. In particular, it's impossible to have instantaneous, virtually no-cost access to unlimited quantities of the highest-quality business intelligence from internal and external sources.

As illustrated in Exhibit 4.2, cost, speed, quantity, and quality are orthogonal qualities, and it's up to management to define the compromise that must be established among the four variables. For example, if management decides that speed—rapid access to

EXHIBIT 4.2

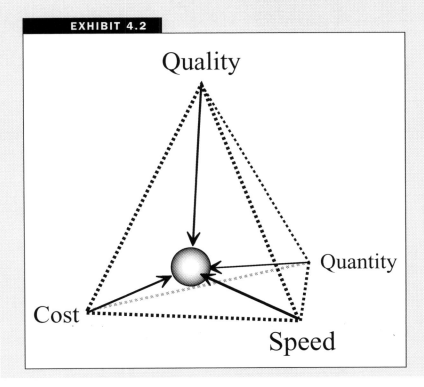

85

ESSENTIALS of XBRL

IN THE REAL WORLD CONTINUED

data—is the highest priority, then the cost is likely to be very high, quality won't be as great as it could be, and the quantity of data will likely be limited by the lack of time. The compromise scenario represented by the exhibit favors low cost, high speed, and quantity of data at the expense of data quality.

The configuration of the pyramidal structure assumes a fixed technology and ignores issues such as shifting economies of scale. The particular mix of cost, speed, quantity, and quality is a reflection of the technology available or readily affordable. For example, shifting from paper-based accounting to computer-based accounting methods is likely to increase cost—at least initially—but eventually it will result in increased speed, quantity, and quality of data. In other words, the pyramid may shrink in response to the incorporation of new technology. Similarly, adding XBRL to the mix has the potential to further contract the axes of the pyramid.

Of course, contraction of the axes is the best-case scenario. For example, it's possible that the new technology is expensive, doesn't scale very well, and introduces errors in the data. In this scenario, the bounds of the pyramidal model expand. The challenge for management is to make decisions that not only reduce or maintain the bounds of cost, speed, quantity, and quality but that provide a mix that is ideally suited to the needs of the corporation.

- The ideal mix of data timeliness, quality, and quantity is a function of the manager's needs.
- The data from disparate sources must be in a form that can be easily identified and consumed.

These and related concepts are expanded in the following sections.

Control

For managers to exercise internal control, they require not only data but a means of accessing the appropriate data when they're needed. It isn't enough to have the data "somewhere in the system" or available only after requesting a report that will take weeks to run. Similarly, the appropriate filters or selection criteria must be able to be used to select the desired data from the undesired data. As the web demonstrates, having millions of Web pages on different topics seems ideal until someone has to wade through hundreds of false answers to a search query to find data relevant to the problem at hand.

Regardless of how the data are generated or the language used to communicate values from one part of the enterprise to the next, the flow of financial data in most companies resembles the pattern illustrated in Exhibit 4.3. As shown, the various transactions and operations of the corporation are the source of data. Because these corporate operations may be geographically disparate and the transactions may occur in different countries using different currencies and tax rates, repre-

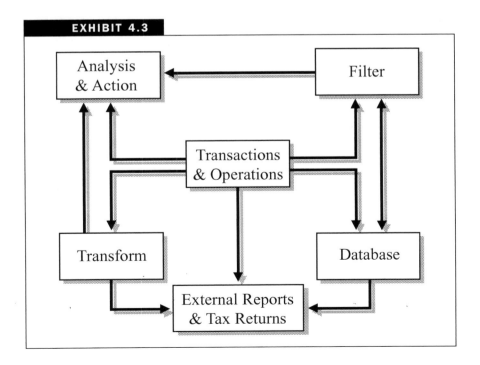

EXHIBIT 4.3

sented on different software packages running on different hardware, it's likely that the systems don't communicate with each other transparently. In other words, the data are likely unstructured and only loosely integrated with each other.

Assuming that the corporation is involved in widget manufacturing, there are financial transactions with suppliers of raw materials, insurance companies, labor, shipping, and management. Furthermore, there are operations relating to the processing and storage of the widgets that generate financial data. Once generated, the data may be stored in a database for later retrieval, filtered or simplified for internal management control, or transformed into a form more appropriate for analysis. The data also may be used directly or indirectly for external reports and tax returns.

As illustrated in the simplified data flow diagram in Exhibit 4.4, much of the process of handling financial data is necessary for fulfilling external reporting requirements and tax obligations. For example, as illustrated in the exhibit, there are four major paths to fulfill external requirements. One path leads to the corporate database, which serves as the long-term memory of transactions and operations. From here, external reports can be generated directly. Another route for reporting data is through a filter before the data are stored in the database in preparation for external reporting. The filter is used to remove data that are unnecessary for outside agencies, such as low-level tracking data on the production of individual units. Another major route for data in the enterprise is through a transform operation, such as statistical analysis and calculations, such as net present value (NPV) and internal rate of return (IRR), intended for external reports for stockholders.

Compared with the processing required for external reporting, the additional data paths for internal management control are minimal. As illustrated in Exhibit 4.5, the major additions are data paths associated with data analysis.

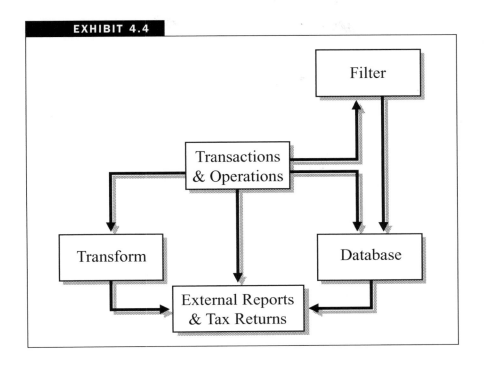

EXHIBIT 4.4

Filter

Transactions
& Operations

Transform

Database

External Reports
& Tax Returns

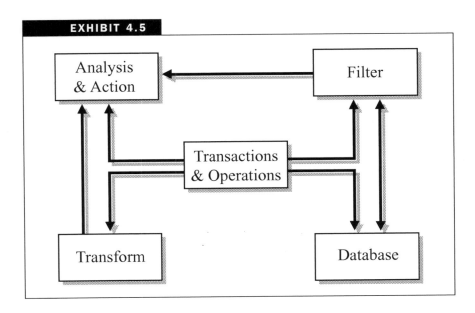

EXHIBIT 4.5

Analysis
& Action

Filter

Transactions
& Operations

Transform

Database

The data relevant to financial reporting that are transported through the corporation information infrastructure may take one or more of the paths shown in Exhibit 4.6, as a function of the varied needs of management. Data from transactions and operations may be analyzed directly (Exhibit 4.6A), after they have been transformed by mathematical operations and formatting (Exhibit 4.6B), or after filtering to simplify the data and remove unwanted details (Exhibit 4.6C). Filtering also may occur after the data have been stored in the corporate database (Exhibit 4.6D).

As shown in Exhibit 4.7, the reports required by management for control of the corporation fall into one of three major categories: Specific Reports, Periodic Limited Reports, and Periodic Comprehensive Reports. Each of these reports, which are all manager specific, is more

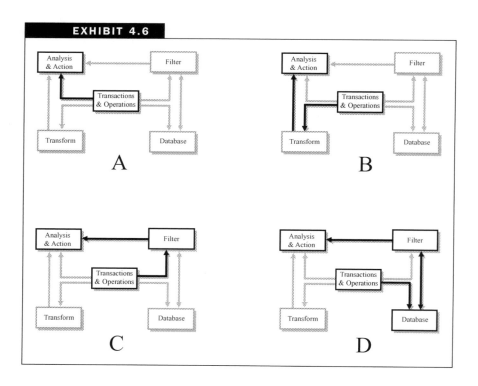

EXHIBIT 4.6

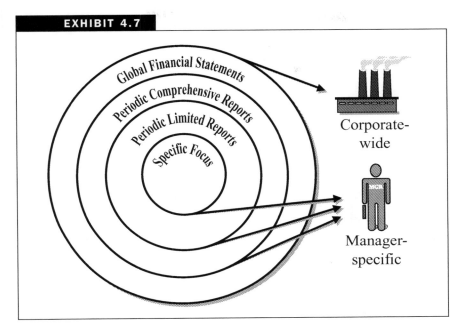

EXHIBIT 4.7

Global Financial Statements

Periodic Comprehensive Reports

Periodic Limited Reports

Specific Focus

Corporate-wide

Manager-specific

focused and more specialized than the global financial statements intended for consumption by outside investors and the government. The most highly filtered reports are Specific Reports that are designed to suit the specific authority and responsibility of a particular manager.

For example, a manager in charge of widget production at one of the corporation's plants might require a report that details: production quantities; shrinkage; number of units lost or damaged; the cost of materials, electrical energy, and human resources required to construct the widgets; the number of widgets in boxes ready for shipment; and the backlog of orders. Acquiring the level of detail necessary for a Specific Report may require a data path with no filtering from the data source (as in Exhibit 4.6A) in cases where there's a single production assembly line.

The next level of control reporting is Periodic Limited Reports, which are intended for a higher-level manager who isn't concerned with the finer details of a Specific Focus Report. Periodic Limited

Reports are useful to managers whose authority and responsibilities are broader. For example, a manager in charge of widget production internationally isn't concerned with the number of widgets damaged at a particular plant but with the summary figures companywide. In this case, a data path similar to B and/or C in Exhibit 4.6 is likely more applicable, because data must be filtered and/or summarized.

At the senior management level, Periodic Comprehensive Reports—executive summaries of corporate-wide activity—are most useful. For example, the profit and cash flow generated by widgets production corporation-wide may be of interest to senior management, but not the lower level detail of what's happening at an individual plant. This view from the top might show comprehensive financial figures related to the production of widgets and all other devices sold by the corporation.

The processes and technologies that should be used to process the data are determined by how the various levels of reporting interrelate and the report types required for management control. Of the technologies available to handling the potentially millions of data points that exist throughout the corporation, a variety of data management processes are available. Of these processes, knowledge management is one of the most synergistic with XBRL tagging of data for internal and external financial reporting.

Knowledge Management

Knowledge management is a deliberate, systematic business optimization strategy that involves the selection, distillation, storage, organization, and communication of data. It's one of the most effective ways of managing unstructured data that are destined for internal control reports and external reports.

The typical KM process is illustrated in Exhibit 4.8. Note that the flow of data is virtually identical to that traditionally used with unstructured, untagged data, as shown in Exhibit 4.3. Although the stages have

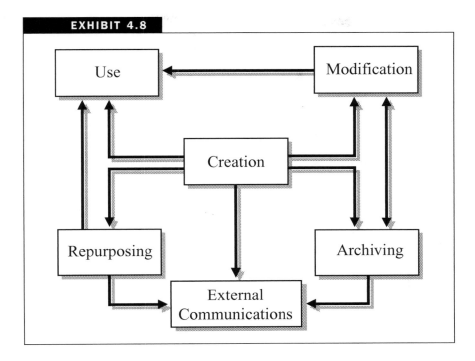

EXHIBIT 4.8

different names, the actions associated with each stage differ mainly in specificity. For example, in the context of financial reporting, the analysis and action phase of unstructured data management is equivalent to the use stage in generic knowledge management. Similarly, while knowledge management deals with external communications, the external communications focus in financial reporting is in the generation of external reports and tax returns.

Beyond labeling the underlying processes at each phase, the superficial differences in the naming of each stage in the management processes are insignificant. However, there are several important distinctions between KM and traditional, unstructured data management that are not evident in the data flow diagrams. For example, data become information and knowledge when a structure is imposed on them. Exhibit 4.9 summarizes the differences between unstructured data management and knowledge management.

EXHIBIT 4.9

Unstructured Data Management	Knowledge Management
Use of Technology	
To integrate data	To facilitate collaboration
To design tables	To create metadata
Use of Standards	
For location mapping	For a controlled vocabulary
Use of Assets	
To make capital investments	To pay knowledge workers
To accrue inventory	To accrue data
Use of Management	
To distribute expertise	To centralize expertise
Culture	
Product focused	Data focused
Production rewarded	Intellectual property rewarded

Knowledge management technology focuses on interpersonal collaboration in the workplace as opposed to integration of data within a computer-based information system. Another technological difference between KM and data management is how data are represented in the underlying information system to reflect this difference in focus. The KM process involves organizing data using hierarchical metadata. Metadata reveal the context in which data are used and are the basis for how the data are represented when they are stored in the underlying databases.

In this regard, XBRL, which supports a hierarchical, metadata structure, is ideally suited to support the KM process. As illustrated in Exhibit 4.10, XBRL can be used to implement a standard vocabulary that reflects the hierarchical data structures used in KM. This use of a standard vocabulary—in this example, the tagging of payroll from different plants within the corporation—is much more flexible than mapping locations within tables in different databases. This flexibility is especially apparent when the databases use different, incompatible database engines that are running on different, incompatible hardware.

Another major difference between traditional data management and KM is the process and contexts in which KM methods are applied—that

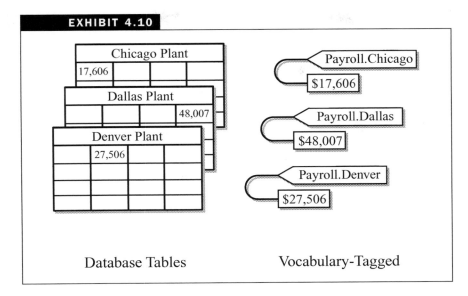

EXHIBIT 4.10

Chicago Plant			
17,606			

Dallas Plant			
		48,007	

Denver Plant			
27,506			

Payroll.Chicago
$17,606

Payroll.Dallas
$48,007

Payroll.Denver
$27,506

Database Tables   Vocabulary-Tagged

is, the corporate culture. A corporation that fully embraces the KM process not only abides by certain principles of manipulating, managing, and accessing data but rewards the creation and management of intellectual property. Whether it's in the form of data in a database or expertise in an employee or "knowledge worker," intellectual property is treated as a valued corporate asset. Furthermore, the corporation tends to be data focused as opposed to product focused.

The approach to managing data also differs in the standards used to provide the basis for control and consistency of data. The most significant standard in a KM system is the controlled vocabulary used to index, archive, and retrieve information and the network protocols and architecture that allow interoperability of different information systems in large corporations. In addition, management is focused on providing support and direction for knowledge workers. Management often takes the form of a centralized chief knowledge officer as opposed to expertise distributed throughout the enterprise.

Knowledge management has its roots in relating disparate data types—taking data from one system within the corporation and combining it with data from another. As such, the major work may be in the modification stage of the KM process, in which data are combined in new ways with a variety of data management utilities. The use of a standard vocabulary, while providing system integration within the corporation, doesn't necessarily facilitate communications with outside vendors or governmental agencies. A KM system may work perfectly within a closed environment, but unless the vocabulary is standardized against external norms, the external reporting functionality can be extremely difficult.

In this regard, XBRL represents a key component in external communications compatibility within the financial reporting arena. Although a functional, corporate-wide control structure could be developed with XML using a proprietary tagging vocabulary and indexing schemes, it could be a waste of resources. A better approach is to standardize on a process that fulfills both the internal and the external reporting processes. Of course, this is easiest where there are no legacy systems with which to contend. In practice, legacy systems and processes can't simply be discarded and replaced by a new system, especially in a multinational, geographically disparate organization. Even so, having a clear vision of how XBRL and the related components of a KM infrastructure can improve corporate competitiveness can help direct decisions moving forward.

Beyond Financial Reporting

If the only application of XBRL were as a facilitator of internal control and external financial reporting process, it would be worth embracing as a means of improving corporate competitiveness. However, the utility of XBRL extends beyond reporting. For example, as described above, XBRL can be used to support the corporate-wide knowledge management process. It does this in several ways. The primary means is by providing a vehicle for allowing the interoperability of disparate computer systems. XBRL, together with an appropriate network infra-structure, such as the Internet, makes it possible for applications to share data, regardless of the software that generates the data or the database that is its source.

Another method by which XBRL can enhance the knowledge management process is by forcing the corporate information services department to confront the issues of Internet- and intranet-based serv-ices that are related to the typical XBRL infrastructure. These include security, privacy, bandwidth limitations of current cables and wireless systems, server space, Web browser compatibility issues, Internet-use monitoring systems, and firewalls to stop hackers and viruses.

XBRL promises to revolutionize business processes along the entire financial information supply chain, from public and private companies, the accounting profession, and regulators, to analysts, the investment community, capital markets, and lenders. Several key third parties, such as software developers and data aggregators, will be affected as well. For example, consider that XBRL and the associated network technologies make it possible for everyday investors to use intelligent agents—soft-ware programs that can search for data on their own—to compile sta-tistics and perform analyses on entire industries or sectors of the econ-omy with the click of a mouse.

The same technology has revolutionized the e-commerce market, where customers can perform a search for the cheapest item on the Internet. Once the item has been defined, a software agent will ferret out the top four or five vendors with the lowest price and present the list to the potential consumer—for the cost of viewing an advertise-ment. Obviously, the role of middlemen in the new XBRL-enabled financial information supply chain will shift considerably once XBRL-compatibility is commonplace.

One of the advantages of using XBRL is that it improves access to selected corporate data by outside investment firms, analysts, and potential individual investors. This improved access is partially due to XBRL's compatibility with the Internet, in that a report represented in XBRL can be easily converted to a standard HTML document on the corporate website, on an investment banker's desktop, or on a manager's wireless personal digital assistant (PDA). In addition, a variety of analytical tools can be applied to the data represented by an XBRL document. XBRL can be used as a facilitator in management's decision-making process, in part because of the relative ease of filtering and locating data. However, the decision support potential of XBRL isn't limited to reports: XBRL also can leverage the data on the Internet. Consider, for example, how a potential investor or the chief executive of a corporation could utilize an integrated view of corporate performance in the context of not only the production and profit of the competition but by geographical region around the globe, by the demographics of the customers served by the company's products. In this sense, XBRL represents the greatest opportunity for the financial and accounting communities to redefine themselves since the introduction of the electronic spreadsheet.

XBRL is a major step forward in facilitating the intra- and inter-corporate communications process. However, the use of XBRL or any other language doesn't solve issues regarding openness, integration, security, business logic, workflow, or user interface design that must be addressed by other technologies and processes. Chapter 5 covers these issues and discusses XBRL from a technology perspective.

Summary

In addition to fulfilling financial reporting obligations, management relies on regular, internal reports to determine the health of the corporation. The key internal reports—Special Focus, Periodic Limited, and Periodic Comprehensive Reports—differ in granularity, focus, and target audience. At the lowest level of granularity are Special Focus

Reports, whereas the Periodic Comprehensive Reports contain high-level, comprehensive views of corporate activity. All of these reports can be generated automatically from the same core data using XBRL. What's more, XBRL can facilitate the timeliness, quantity, and quality of data, based on the manager's particular requirements and cost constraints. On a larger scale, XBRL can be used as a facilitator for a knowledge management process that not only focuses on financial data but extends through the technological and cultural fabric of the company.

Do not be desirous of having things done quickly. Do not look at small advantages. Desiring to have things done quickly prevents their being done thoroughly. Looking at small advantages prevents great affairs from being accomplished.

—Confucius

CHAPTER 5

Technology

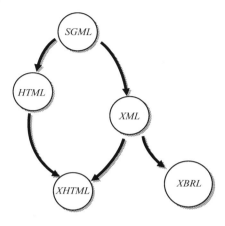

After reading this chapter you will be able to

- Appreciate the historical context of XBRL and its relationship with XML

- Understand the high-level technical underpinnings of XBRL

- Appreciate XBRL as an enabling technology for a variety of applications in financial reporting

This chapter explores XBRL from a perspective appropriate for a chief executive or other senior manager with some familiarity with desktop or laptop personal computer (PC) systems. In particular, this chapter provides a historical context for the development of XBRL in the evolution of computer hardware, software, the publishing industry, and the World Wide Web over the latter half of the 20th century. It also examines XBRL as a variation of its parent language, eXtensible Markup Language (XML). The technical applications of XBRL are discussed as well as the major approaches to providing an infrastructure capable of supporting XBRL reporting. Finally, the chapter explores the potential future directions of the accounting profession once XBRL-enabled technologies become commonplace.

Context

One of the most important technological innovations since our ancestors discovered how to create and control fire was the creation of written languages. The modern concept of writing had a humble beginning over 15,000 years ago, in the form of a number notation in which scratches and notches were arranged in groups of straight lines to represent the passage of time and other quantities. Ten thousand years later, in the area now known as the Middle East, the notches were replaced with an alphabet that was inscribed on clay tablets by the intelligentsia, including the first accountants, to record legal contracts, tax assessments, sales, and the census to show who owed and paid taxes. Over time, thousands of clay tablets accumulated, forming the first library. Like the use of Latin during the Dark Ages, the primitive language went beyond oral communications and served as a common or intermediary language that could be used to translate among the various languages that developed over the next few thousand years.

Today the Department of Defense libraries, the National Library of Congress, and the National Archives are three of the most notable libraries out of over 130,000 libraries in the United States. Many of these libraries rely on the Dewey Decimal System for classifying their holdings and to make it easier for patrons to retrieve information from a written index or computerized database. The Dewey Decimal System is a method for arranging nonfiction books by subject in a consistent and logical numerical order. Books are assigned to one of 10 subject categories, and each category is allotted 100 numbers, with each number referring to a specific topic. The result is a taxonomy or hierarchy of topics—a concept that is fundamental to XBRL.

Consider the Dewey Decimal taxonomy for finance illustrated in Exhibit 5.1. The taxonomy can be considered a tree structure, with a root, branches, and leaves. In the exhibit, "Social sciences" is the root and "Economics" is one of nine major branches. From this branch are nine minor branches, including "Financial economics." Finally, one of the thousands of potentially unlimited leaves of this branch is "History of money." Although not visible in the exhibit, each of the 10 major categories branches into 10 other branches. Similarly, each of these branches leads to 10 other branches. As a result, there are $10 \times 10 \times 10$, or 1,000, terminal branches that may be populated with a virtually unlimited number of leaves. In addition, several books may share the same leaf designation. For example, in the exhibit, there may be one or 100 books categorized under "332.4 History of money." Furthermore, the taxonomy can be extended by extending the numerical code ad infinitum, as in 332.41, 332.401, or 332.4258.

Some libraries still use an indexed paper card catalog to identify the location of books—a system reminiscent of the catalogs used by the librarians of antiquity. However, things started to get interesting when

EXHIBIT 5.1

000 Generalities			
100 Philosophy	310 General statistics		
200 Religion	320 Political science	331 Labor economics	
300 Social sciences ——	**330 Economics** ——	**332 Financial economics** ——	**332.4 History of money**
400 Language	340 Law	333 Land economics	
500 Natural sciences	350 Public administration	334 Cooperatives	
600 Technology	360 Social services	335 Socialism	
700 The arts	370 Education	336 Public finance	
800 Literature	380 Commerce	337 International economics	
900 Geography	390 Customs	338 Production	
		339 Macroeconomics	

librarians began using computerized catalogs, indexed by the Dewey Decimal System as well as author, title, and topic. Computers have not only revolutionized how the typical library manages data on its holding; they have revolutionized how the books and other collections of data are created.

Computers

The electronic computer, a classified technology developed during the 1930s and 1940s, initially was used primarily for military applications, from weapons systems design and control to message encryption and code breaking. When the technology was made available for commercial consumption after World War II, there was no interface to help computer users make sense of the data. Output consisted of seemingly endless strings of alphanumerical data that were essentially meaningless to someone without training. To increase the readability of text displayed on computer consoles, a variety of computer-specific control codes were developed to format a document in a specific way. For example, document titles could be centered and the beginning of paragraphs could be indented automatically. Since these proprietary codes, such as "<Format-12>", were embedded in the document, a document created on one computer system often couldn't be displayed on another computer system, because control codes weren't standardized. The code "<Format-12>", besides having no intuitive meaning, might be interpreted as "center text" on one computer system and "double space" on another.

To facilitate the sharing of electronic documents, engineers from the computer industry, publishers, designers, and others involved electronic documents pushed to replace system-specific text formatting or markup codes with standard codes. The term "markup" came from the printing industry, where proofreaders marked formatting and correction codes on page proofs that were then typeset. The first widely recognized standard

Tools of the Trade

Few in the financial and accounting industries doubt that moving to Web-based reporting will restructure the value chain and redefine the accounting profession. Part of this transformation will include the routine use of information technologies that can be applied to XBRL-based financial data. One class of tools is intelligent agents, software robots that perform routine tasks, such as searching for a company that fits a certain criterion. These programs, first popularized for locating products and services from the thousands of e-commerce sites on the web, are easy to apply to XBRL documents. Some of the advantages of using intelligent agents over manual methods include time savings, freedom from having to define explicit and often lengthy search criterion, and freedom from errors due to misspellings and omission of search terms.

A central issue for professionals in the accounting industry is who will use these Web-enabled tools: accounting professionals or end users. This concern that some clients may bypass accounting services and interact directly with analysis tools is understandable, given how the web has transformed many other industries. For example, when reservations for the airlines industry were first integrated under the American Airlines' SABRE (Semi-Automated Business Research Environment) computer reservation system, access to electronic data was limited to internal airline staff and affiliated travel agents. However, with the move from a closed electronic data interchange (EDI) system to an open Web-based system, more adventuresome customers began bypassing travel agents. Mainstream travelers quickly moved to use the web for self-booking as soon as the major travel agencies began charging consumers for their services. The exodus was further encouraged by the advent of intelligent agents that allowed travelers to find the best price from the various online reservation systems in a few minutes with only a few mouse clicks.

It's easy to envision a scenario where a potential investor uses an intelligent agent to search through the financials of every company listed on Nasdaq and to automatically compile a list of companies with the greatest quarterly or annual profits, cash flow, or other criteria established by the investor. The same technology could be applied to internal reports to determine the most appropriate course of action in order to maximize corporate profit, liquidity, or cash flow, depending on the manager's objectives.

As shown in Exhibit 5.2, there is no shortage of intelligent agents or search engines that can be applied to financial reporting data on the web or a corporate intranet. Some products are designed to reside locally on a PC, whereas others are freely available on the web. The major issues, once financial data are available for

EXHIBIT 5.2

Technologies	Examples
Intelligent agents (Desktop)	Intelliseek
	Copernic
	Lexibot
	WebFerret
	SearchPad
	WebStorm
	NetAttache
Intelligent agents (Web)	Dogpile
	Ixquick
	MetaCrawler
	QbSearch
	ProFusion
	SurfWax
	Vivisimo
Search engines (Desktop)	AskMe
	Cadenza
Search engines (Public)	Google
	Lycos
	Yahoo!
	Excite
	AltaVista
	AllTheWeb
	CompletePlanet

was the Generalized Markup Language (GML), introduced in the late 1960s (see Exhibit 5.3). GML was used heavily on IBM mainframe computer systems to format and control data destined for print publishing.

With an increasing number of computer vendors in the rapidly expanding worldwide computer market in the 1970s, the need for an international standard became evident. In 1978, on the heels of the introduction of the PC and at the same time the electronic spreadsheet was introduced, the American National Standards Institute (ANSI) formed a committee to define the Special Generalized Markup Language (SGML), a markup language specification based on GML. By 1983 there were sev-

EXHIBIT 5.3

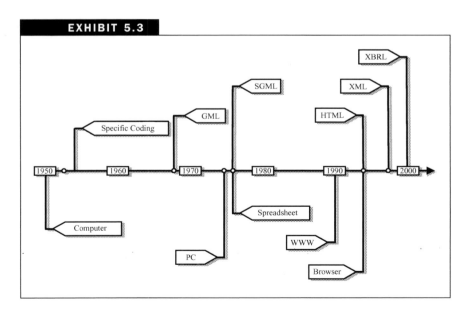

eral major adopters of SGML, including the U.S. Internal Revenue Service and the U.S. Department of Defense. In 1984 SGML acquired the backing of the International Organization for Standardization (ISO). A year later it was adopted by the Office of Official Publications of the European Community. Since then SGML has been embraced by the Association of American Publishers (AAP) for applications such as the interchange of manuscripts between authors and their publishers.

Aside from excitement at a few academic institutions where computer-science types were aware of the graphical user interface (GUI) concepts pioneered at Xerox's Palo Alto Research Center (PARC) and popularized by introduction of the Apple Macintosh in 1984, the debut of the graphical World Wide Web in 1990 was accompanied by little fanfare. The few consumers and businesspeople who were aware of the web saw it as little more than a GUI to the unfamiliar network called the Internet. Things changed for businesses and consumers in 1993 with the availability of the first-generation Web browsers and, most important, the first version of the Hypertext Markup Language (HTML), which allowed anyone with modest computer skills to author Web pages. Within a year there was a rush for dot-com addresses, and every major business, scientist, and artist had to have a Web presence—typically little more than an electronic billboard—or risk missing out on another broadcast medium.

In 1998, near the height of the dot-com boom, version 1.0 of the eXtensible Markup Language (XML) was released as a means of producing interactive Web pages that could be used to process transactions, access databases, and share data between applications. XML was embraced almost immediately by hundreds of vendors, organizations, and individuals and modified or extended to suit their needs. Representatives from the accounting industry were among the early adopters of XML, and they created a prototype language called Extensible Financial Reporting Markup Language (XFRML). By 2000, version 1.0 of the language was released, renamed the eXtensible Business Reporting Language (XBRL).

Before delving into the specifics of XBRL, which is simply XML with a customized taxonomy, a review of the basics of computer languages is in order.

Languages

A language is a system of communication with its own set of conventions and special words. Most languages have a specific syntax, grammar, and vocabulary. Grammar is the system of rules by which words are formed and put together to make sentences, and syntax is the part of grammar that deals with the arrangement and ordering of words in a sentence. Vocabulary is the collection of all the words contained in a language, as represented by a dictionary. In most languages, the syntax and grammar are fixed, but the vocabulary normally changes with time, as users of the language need to express new concepts and as old concepts fall out of use. The government of the country of origin tightly controls some languages, such as French, where the vocabulary can be expanded only periodically and only after considerable debate. Other languages, such as American English, seem to expand daily, especially in the marketing of new technology products and services.

Computer languages differ from languages such as French or English primarily in that they are not intended for human conversation. They are further distinguished by their computer-specific applications and their associated characteristics. For example, most computer languages can be categorized as either declarative or procedural. An example of a declarative statement is:

Income = $43,212.14; Loss = $43,000.00

In contrast, an example of a procedural statement is:

Profit = Income − Expenses; Print Profit

XML and, by extension, XBRL are declarative languages, in that they describe data. They don't say anything about what should be done with the data but simply describe "what is." In the declarative statement above, values are assigned to Income and Loss. After that, the interpretation is up to the computer program that manipulates the income and loss values.

In contrast, computer languages such as C and COBOL are procedural, meaning that they are used to specify the sequence of operations that the computer must follow to accomplish a specific task—otherwise known as a program. The procedural statement above tells the computer to subtract expenses from income and print the resulting profit figure. The characteristics associated with declarative and procedural languages are summarized in Exhibit 5.4.

Procedural (programming) languages such as C, Java, BASIC, and COBOL are often used to create high-performance applications, such as database management systems, word processing programs, and electronic spreadsheets. Performance, measured as relative speed of execution against industry-wide benchmarks, is typically high for an application written in a procedural language because the procedural statements—the source code—is compiled. That is, the source code (language that a programmer creates) is subject to a one-time process in which the procedural statements are converted by a computer program

EXHIBIT 5.4

	Declarative	Procedural
Example	XML, XBRL	C, JAVA
Validation	Easy	Difficult
Perspective	Data	Process
Extensibility	Easy	Difficult
Performance	Low	High
Execution	External	Self

into a set of low-level machine instructions that can be saved as an executable file or program. When the program, such as a word processor or spreadsheet, is needed, it can be fed directly to the computer hardware for immediate execution.

In contrast, most declarative languages, such as XML, are interpreted. Every time a program that uses the declarative statements in an XBRL document is run, each declarative statement must be converted, one statement at a time, into a set of machine instructions that are in turn executed on the computer hardware. It's important to note that XBRL code isn't interpreted by itself but must be acted on by an external program, just as a compiler program acts on the source code written in a procedural language.

Because of the way XML is constructed and interpreted, it's relatively easy to extend with additional vocabulary and to validate the statements—akin to spell-checking and grammar-checking a document in Microsoft Word. The extensions added to XML usually can be validated relatively quickly and easily by virtue of the interactive interpretation process. Adding additional words to the XML vocabulary and modifying the taxonomy simply entails adding tags to an XML document. In contrast, new words typically can't be added to a program created by a procedural language without editing and recompiling the original source code. Furthermore, the source code is virtually never available. Even if it is available, compiled languages require more time and effort to debug or validate than interpreted declarative languages because of the relatively lengthy compile-edit-run-edit-recompile process. For example, the typical reader wouldn't be able to modify the spell-checker function in Microsoft Word without the source code, and asking Microsoft to make the change isn't likely to result in action.

In the early 1980s, a programming paradigm called object-oriented programming (OOP) became popular because it allowed programmers to hide and therefore more easily manage the increasing complexity of procedural programs. The key elements in the object-oriented paradigm are objects, which are software packets that contain a collection of procedures and data. Objects belong to classes, which describe characteristics of similar objects. An object belonging to a particular class, called an instance of that class, inherits the properties of that class. Another component of the object-oriented paradigm is that objects communicate with each other through messages.

As a concrete example of an object-oriented paradigm, consider a tree or hierarchy in which a car sits at the root. Branching from the root are components of the car—the main chassis, the tires, and the engine. Any other tire can be described in terms of tires on the car. They may be whitewalls instead of black, a different diameter or width, and perhaps with a different tread. A programmer who needs to describe a new tire doesn't have to start from scratch but can define a new tire by defining the exceptions to the original car tires.

Object-oriented languages, exemplified by Java and C++, hide complexity by encapsulating procedures in objects, which belong to classes that can be modified incrementally through inheritance. For example, in Exhibit 5.5, objects are arranged in an inheritance hierarchy or tree, with "Analysis" at the root. Following the "Profit" branch to the "Net" branch, an instance of the Net Profit object, forms a leaf of the tree. The sender, an "Income" object that is part of another tree, sends a message—the income value, or $1,456,980—to the Net Profit instance, which returns the Net Profit value ($37,102). A programmer using the object-oriented approach doesn't have to deal with the logic or formulas associated with calculating liquidity but only with which objects' messages are valid.

Despite the overhead of having to maintain each of the objects in a tree, the advantage of an object-oriented programming language is that the details are hidden from view until they are needed. Furthermore, once a library of objects has been created, the objects can be easily

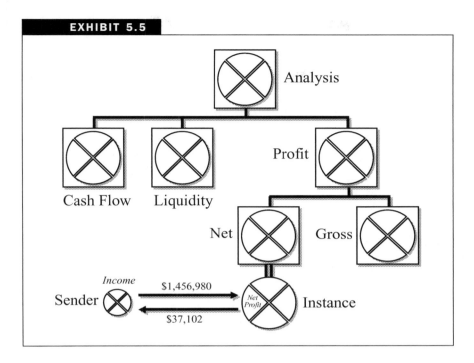

EXHIBIT 5.5

repurposed for other applications. Although XML isn't considered a true object-oriented language, it and some of its associated utilities borrow many of the concepts of the object-oriented paradigm, such as the tree structure and the use of instances. With this brief review of computer languages, now consider XML and XBRL in more detail.

XML

XML doesn't have a predefined vocabulary or taxonomy. Instead, the vocabulary and the relationship of the vocabulary words with each other and the document (the taxonomy) are defined as declarations are made. As a result, any system of declarations created in XML can reasonably be considered XML. However, to distinguish one system of declarations from another, they are often renamed. For example, the Extensible Business Reporting Markup Language (XBRL) and Electronic Business Extensible Markup Language (ebXML) used in business, the Bioinformatic Sequence Markup Language (BSML) and Genome Annotation Markup Elements (GAME) used in molecular biology, and the Extensible Markup Language—Message Text Format (XML-MTF) used by the U.S. armed forces are all XML. The name of each version of XML really refers to its unique taxonomy. The following discussion applies equally to XBRL as it does to any other extension of XML.

Although XML is being applied to a variety of applications in dozens of industries, it had humble beginnings as a language developed expressly to support e-commerce on the web. One of the motivations for creating XML was to overcome the shortcomings of the web's original language, Hypertext Markup Language (HTML). Unlike XML, HTML doesn't distinguish between data and their presentation. Furthermore, HTML deals only with the appearance of data, not their meaning. An HTML statement that declares the color of the word "car" to be red isn't treated differently from a statement that declares the color of the word "apple" to be red. Both "car" and "apple" are simply words or text strings, with no meaning or context.

HTML isn't extensible by users, but the vocabulary must be expanded incrementally by the World Wide Web Consortium (W3C) committee—a lengthy process that is akin to adding to the official French vocabulary. Furthermore, once a new version of HTML has been officially sanctioned, the extensions have to be incorporated in the major Web browsers, which will interpret the HTML declarative statements on each user's PC. Because of the time lag between the introduction of a new version of HTML and the widespread availability of browsers that can understand declarations made in the new version, there have only been a handful of versions with vocabulary extensions since HTML was introduced. Furthermore, since there are still many older browsers in use, many of which may not be compatible with the latest release of HTML, Web content developers often avoid using the latest HTML tags to ensure that the program content can be displayed on older browsers.

A comparison of XML and HTML (as in Exhibit 5.6) reveals several similarities and a few marked differences. In terms of similarities, both are declarative languages, in that an external procedural language must act on their statements in order to have any effect. For example, an HTML statement that specifies the color of a given text string doesn't automatically color the text; the HTML interpreter in a Web browser that processes the HTML statement must accomplish the action. Similarly, an XML statement that declares the value of a variable doesn't actually assign the value to a variable. This assignment must be accomplished by a procedural language, such as Java, running on a server or in a Java-compatible Web browser, such as the latest version of Microsoft's Internet Explorer or Netscape Navigator. The data declarations in an XML document may never be displayed but rather are used as a database or communicated between disparate computer systems.

Much of the data on the current web is trapped out of context in HTML forms. Although search engines can locate some of this data, for the most part, it is unusable by other applications, because HTML documents provide little, if any, context to the data they contain. Search engines treat the word "medallion," rendered in gold text, in the same way they treat the word "medallion" rendered in red. The search engines

---

EXHIBIT 5.6

	XML (XBRL)	HTML
Language	Declarative	Declarative
Data & display	Separate	Combined
Perspective	Data	Display
Extensibility	By user/developer	By committee
Computer manipulation	Easy	Difficult
Execution	Stand-alone procedural Language or Web browser	Web browser
Structured by	Data	Display
Search	Context specific	Nonspecific

make no inference that the gold color may indicate a gold medal or medallion and that the reference in red may refer to a piece of beef. In contrast, XML, used either alone or in conjunction with HTML, can be used to create Web pages that not only look good but can be automatically searched, manipulated, and transformed into a variety of other forms because the data are structured according to context.

Exhibit 5.7 illustrates a popular combination of technologies used to deliver content on the Web. XML documents provide the data, Java provides the processing of the XML declarations, and HTML defines the look of the presentation in the user's browser. Whereas Java's interpretation of XML may occur on a server environment or in the user's browser environment, the interpretation of HTML is performed locally in the user's browser environment, such as Netscape or Internet Explorer.

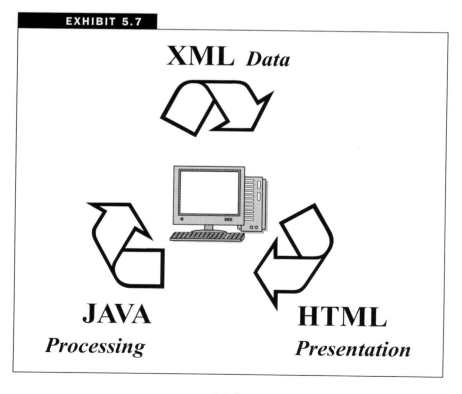

EXHIBIT 5.7

XML *Data*

JAVA
Processing

HTML
Presentation

Data

To better appreciate the utility of XML as a means of defining data for use in a networked environment, consider the architecture of a typical XML document. As shown in Exhibit 5.8, an XML document can be represented as a hierarchy, or tree of nodes. By virtue of this tree structure, XML can be used to store data in a way that lends itself to searching and other forms of automatic computer processing. The tree which provides a structured taxonomy for the data contained in the XML document, can contain seven node types. Of particular relevance to reporting applications are text nodes, element (data) nodes, comment nodes,

EXHIBIT 5.8

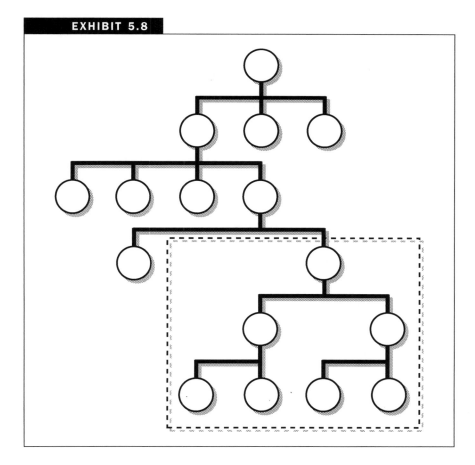

and one root node. The parent-child relatedness of tree branches and nodes lends meaning to the data and establishes a context for them.

It's important to note that the tree structure in Exhibit 5.8 is a *virtual* structure that is defined by the relationships among the tags used in an XML document. That is, the node structure exists only by the virtue of the order and nesting of declarations within the XML document. For example, the seven lower nodes contained in the rectangle in the lower right of the exhibit could be defined in the XML document as:

```
<client>
    <client_address>
        <street >123 Main Street </street>
        <city >Windy City </city>
    </client_address>
    <client_name>
        <first >John </first>
        <last >Doe </last>
    </client_name>
</client>
```

The equivalent tree structure, with labeled nodes, is shown in Exhibit 5.9.

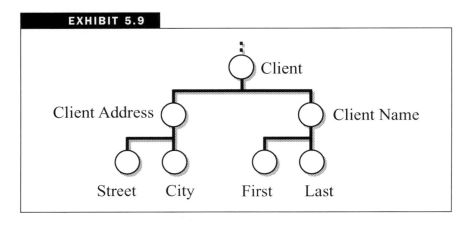

EXHIBIT 5.9

The taxonomy drawn in Exhibit 5.9 lends contextual meaning to the tags used to define the XML document. Consider the "first" tag, indicating first name. Alone and out of context, it could refer to the first of an ordered list, the first in rank, the first in quality, or even first base in baseball. Although XML isn't based on an object-oriented paradigm, it does make use of a hierarchy to provide a context for the data. For example, taken in the context defined by the tree structure, "first" clearly refers to the "first" name of the client. By following the tree toward the root, we may discover that the client name and address are a component of a general ledger document. More important, a computer program written in a procedural language also can infer context from the structure. As a result, a search for "first name" shouldn't return "first" in any context other than first name.

The document that defines the rules for the structure and the content of an XML document is referred to as the schema. The schema not only defines context of specific data but its format as well. For example, the part of the schema that defines the client information taxonomy shown in Exhibit 5.9 may constrain the declaration for the client's last name to a text string of no more than 15 characters. Similarly, numerical data in an XML document may be constrained to dollar exhibits only with no cents, and percentages may be rounded to the nearest percentage point. The structure of XML documents also can be defined by document type definitions (DTDs), which we won't explore, for our purposes, it's sufficient to know that they exist. The point to remember is that a schema acts like a template within an XML document to specify the form that the document should take, and that schema tend to be specific to a document and an industry. That is, the schema differentiates XBRL from ebXML, XML-MTF, and the hundreds of other extensions of XML.

In addition to providing a context for the vocabulary used to tag data, the use of a specific schema for a particular document, such as a corporate general ledger, greatly facilitates the ease with which it can be communicated from one document or computer system to the next. When the schema is known, it's straightforward to map one schema onto another automatically, as in Exhibit 5.10. Schema remapping may involve simply shuffling the expected structure of an XML document from one format to another, without any loss of data. However, as in Exhibit 5.10, the transformation from one schema to another also may involve filtering unwanted or unnecessary data. In the exhibit, the customer information component of the XML document is retained in the new schema but several of the other components of the original schema don't appear.

Display

XML is a versatile language that lends itself to more uses than as a container for structuring data. Because the data in an XML document are tagged hierarchically, they can be efficiently located, manipulated, and transformed into a variety of formats through computational methods. For example, a single XML document can be transformed into another

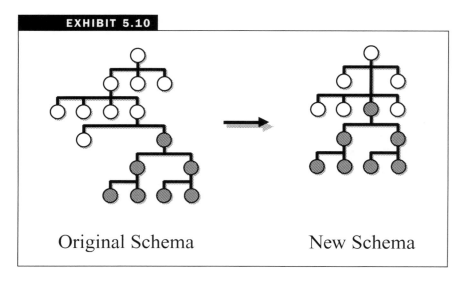

EXHIBIT 5.10

Original Schema   New Schema

XML document with a completely new taxonomy, a document that is compatible with any of the commercial databases, a spreadsheet that is preconfigured to analyze the data, or a document that can be displayed on an XML-compatible Web browser, as depicted in Exhibit 5.11.

The configuration or architecture illustrated in Exhibit 5.11 shows the XML document sent from a Web server over the Internet, where it is transformed on the user's workstation to suit a variety of needs. Focusing on the display of the XML data as a report, we see that a single XML document can provide a variety of reports by virtue of stylesheets.

A stylesheet is a collection of template rules written in an extension of XML called, appropriately, the Extensible Stylesheet Language (XSL). When interpreted by a procedural language, such as Java, a stylesheet can transform the structure of an XML document, amalgamate several XML documents into a single XML or HTML document,

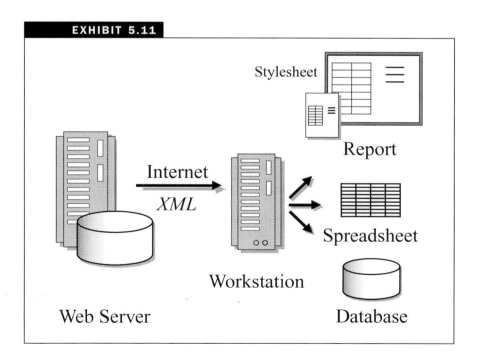

EXHIBIT 5.11

Stylesheet

Report

Internet

XML

Spreadsheet

Workstation

Web Server

Database

or produce several documents from a single XML source file. A stylesheet can define much more than simple document formatting because the XSL has functions for formatting, sorting, concatenating, condition testing (if-then), logical operations (and, or, not), and basic numerical functions (sum, round) that can be interpreted by a procedural language.

Each rule in a stylesheet consists of an association between a pattern of data in the XML document and the processing that should be applied to it for the data to be displayed. In the example in Exhibit 5.12, the stylesheet uses the tagged data on the client's last and first name to define a formatted document with the client's name listed at the top of the document, with last name first. The first name also can be made to appear in the salutation of the formatted document, illustrating how the order of appearance of data in the formatted document isn't limited by order of appearance of data in the XML source document.

Just as the schema of one XML document can be mapped onto the schema of another XML document, the data in an XML document can be mapped onto a variety of formats, as defined by the stylesheets. In the example shown in Exhibit 5.13, a single XML document serves as

EXHIBIT 5.12

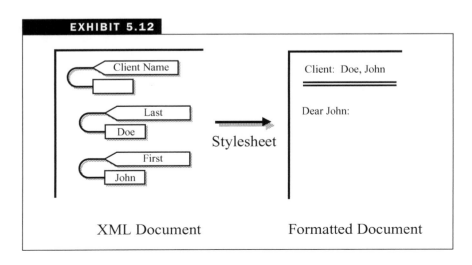

Client Name

Last

Doe

First

John

Stylesheet

Client: Doe, John

Dear John:

XML Document

Formatted Document

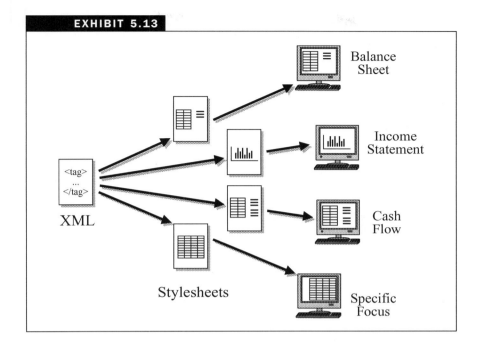

EXHIBIT 5.13

data repository for all major financial data for a corporation, including data on cash flow, profit, liquidity, and the operation of individual divisions and units worldwide. Trying to interpret all of these data at once would likely be overwhelming, but by selecting an appropriate stylesheet, the manager can review the data according to standard business formats, including the balance sheet, income statement, and cash flow, and even look at the operation of a specific plant. Managers accustomed to seeing the profit or loss of the business on the general ledger's bottom line can view the data in that format or in any other format, depending on their choice of stylesheet. The various stylesheets may be defined by an accountant in the company's finance department, an outside accountant, a third-party vendor, or, with the appropriate tools, the chief executive.

There are two basic approaches to apply stylesheets to XML documents. The first, illustrated in Exhibit 5.11, is to have a Web server send XML across the Internet to the client machine, where the stylesheet is processed on the user's PC. The advantage of this approach is that the XML data may be used for a variety of purposes, limited only by the availability of software and processing power on the client machine. The downside of this approach is that the user's workstation has to perform the processing; not only must the workstation have sufficient processing power, but the correct versions of the various software packages must be installed on the workstation to perform the analysis and formatting of the data.

The other basic approach to creating reports for distribution over the Internet or an internal network is to use XML and stylesheets on the server and then make the reports, in the form of HTML documents, available for display on the user's workstation through a standard Web browser (see Exhibit 5.14). This server-side processing offloads software version control and processing overhead to whoever is in charge of running the server. All the user needs to have is a browser capable of displaying HTML. This approach also allows the corporation to maintain

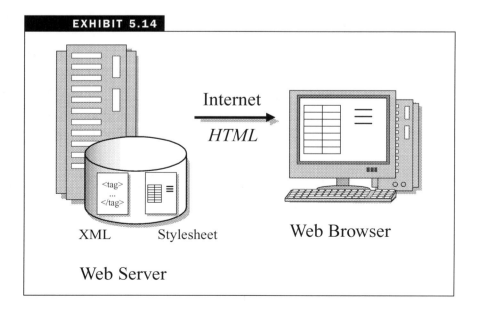

EXHIBIT 5.14

Internet

HTML

XML   Stylesheet

Web Browser

Web Server

a central, secure copy of corporate data and selectively release only those data that it deems appropriate to the intended audience. Chapter 6 explains how both server-side processing and client-side processing of XML documents lend themselves to myriad applications for corporate executives, stockholders, and accounting professionals.

Summary

XBML, as an extension of XML, derives power from its standard schema that defines not only the vocabulary of automatic financial reporting but the hierarchical relationship between the words in the vocabulary. As a declarative language, XBML is lifeless unless acted on by an active procedural or programming language that interprets the declarative statements. This interpretation can occur on a server or on the client machine, depending on the capabilities of the hardware, the control that should be exercised over the data in the XBML source document, and the requirements of the users. As a relatively immature language, the range of possible applications for XBML has yet to be fully explored. However, the applications that have been developed are significant. For example, it's now possible to programmatically transform a single XBML document containing business data into a variety of reports customized for a range of audiences, as well as files that can be read into databases, spreadsheets, decision support tools, and a host of other applications.

The better telescopes become,
The more stars there will be.

—**Gustave Flaubert**

The Human Factor

In the winter of 2002, the president of a major CD (compact disc) duplicating service in Boston received a frantic phone call from the legal representative of a nationally syndicated talk show host. To the celebrity's horror, the latest CD compilation of his talk shows, when played on a CD console or computer connected to the Internet, displayed obscene messages where the talk titles should have been listed. The celebrity, known for his conservative views, was understandably upset, and his attorney threatened to sue everyone in the CD production chain, from the producers to the duplicating service.

Fortunately for the manager of the CD duplication service, he could prove that the master CD wasn't altered in any way after it was received from the program developer. Further searching revealed that there was no virus or alteration on the CD itself. It was discovered that whoever registered the CD compilation with the compact disc data base (CDDB®) service—apparently not a fan of the talk show host—had registered it with an inaccurate list of track titles.

The CDDB service, formally known as the Gracenote CDDB Music Recognition Service, is an Internet-based service licensed to developers of software CD players, CD burners, and other applications. The service allows listeners to view the artist, title, and other information about the contents of a CD when it's played on their PC's built-in CD player. The attraction of the CDDB service is that manufacturers of increasingly popular PC-based CD players can provide added value to listeners, by virtue of a common interconnection to the Internet service.

The incident underscores how features such as automatic, unsupervised updating of data can have disastrous effects when the data are in error. For example, although XBRL allows financial updates to propagate automatically through the financial system,

IN THE REAL WORLD CONTINUED

there must be methods of detecting and correcting errors inadvertently or intentionally introduced into the system. An erroneous financial statistic that is propagated immediately through the financial reporting system can be disastrous for every company in the financial value chain. The moral is that technology doesn't obviate human error or the need to introduce new processes slowly and in a controlled manner.

CHAPTER 6

Solutions

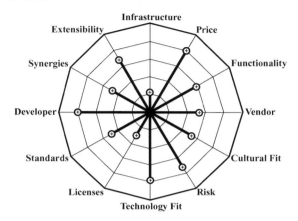

After reading this chapter you will be able to

- Appreciate the real-world solutions that XBRL offers accounting and finance professionals and their clients
- Understand the evaluation criteria for XBRL products
- Understand the risks of adopting an XBRL-based reporting strategy
- Appreciate the time line required for universal XBRL adoption

Every technically savvy senior manager knows that evaluating what appears to be a technological solution to a business problem requires more than simply knowing the technology. Considering a solution that requires an investment in time and other business resources involves an assessment of the business. For example, how can the potential solutions be integrated into the corporate culture? How can the risk of failure be quantified? How can the resources required to provide an adequate infrastructure be identified? Who will do the work of installation and continued maintenance? Within this practical context, this chapter explores how the XBRL-enabled technologies introduced in Chapter 5 can be applied as practical solutions for financial reporting and analysis.

Infrastructure

Solutions to business challenges don't occur in a vacuum but are responses to the affordability, availability, and appropriateness of current technology and business practice. When it comes to evaluating modern technology-based solutions, the most important criteria have to do with the supporting infrastructure. For example, a cell phone or wireless personal digital assistant (PDA) solution to the challenge of maintaining communications between a sales force and the central office is worthless without a wireless services provider that provides robust, reliable, secure, and affordable wireless connectivity to the Internet and public telephone network. Similarly, a personal computer (PC) isn't very useful as a tool to increase employee efficiency and effectiveness of an employee without a network. More important than the desktop PC capabilities is the connectivity to the Internet and corporate intranet for sharing files, sending and receiving e-mail, and accessing shared fax machines and printers.

Similarly, we must consider the information technology (IT) infrastructure that is needed to bring lifeless XBRL statements to life. To better understand the role of XBRL as a solution to business reporting in the context of the available infrastructure technologies, consider the evolution of the IT infrastructure available to the business community and then the web-networked PCs (web services), as outlined in Exhibit 6.1.

Architecture Progression

The most obvious change in IT since the general availability of computers in the 1960s is the progression of computer architecture. The first

| EXHIBIT 6.1 | | | |

IT INFRASTRUCTURE EVOLUTION			
Period	1960s–1980s	1980s–1990s	1990s–Current
Architecture	Mainframe	Client/Server	Web Services
Hardware Platform	Mainframe and Minis	Servers and PCs	Servers and PCs, wireless handsets, tablets, and PDAs
Platform Characteristics	Centralized Homogeneous Controlled	Distributed Homogeneous Controlled	Distributed Mixed Uncontrolled
User Base	Hundreds	Thousands	Multiple thousands
Networks	Closed	Local Area Networks Intranets Internet	Local area networks Intranets Internet Wireless
Data	Proprietary	Proprietary	Proprietary and open
Technologic Hurdles	Performance Operating System	Performance Operating System Security Interfaces	Performance Security Standards 24×7 availability
Users	Programmers Technicians	Data Consumers	Data Consumers
Value	Processing	Connectivity Affordability	Connectivity Interoperability Affordability Remote maintenance

computer architectures were based on room-size monstrosities that required a team of technicians simply to replace the short-lived vacuum tubes that provided the basis for calculations. As shown in Exhibit 6.2, mainframe computers accounted for the lion's share of computer sales from the 1960s and into the 1980s.

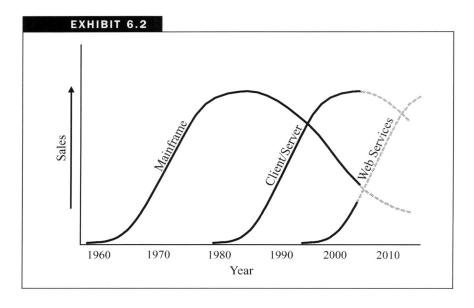

EXHIBIT 6.2

The mainframe computer, named after the main rack or frame that originally housed the massive central processing unit (CPU) of the early vacuum–tube computers, provides a centralized, homogeneous, con-

TIPS & TECHNIQUES

Early Success

Before XML was viewed as a language that could be extended to XBRL for financial reporting, its primary role was in document formatting and electronic publishing. One of the first successful business uses of XML was as a database of electronic components for National Semiconductor. By using the equivalent of stylesheets based on market profiles, the company was able to generate versions of catalogs customized for different markets without modifying the underlying XML document. Customers who received the custom catalogs benefited because they always had up-to-the-minute catalogs containing only those components that pertained to their needs.

trolled, and generally closed infrastructure, as illustrated in Exhibit 6.3. Mainframes concentrate all of the processing power in one location (centralized); the components are all from one manufacturer or at least work as a synchronous whole (homogeneous); the computing environment is completely under the control of the computer operator (controlled); and they aren't made to accept hardware from third parties (closed). Although many large corporations still rely on mainframe computers when raw performance on large databases is required, the price-performance ratio is high for initial cost, maintenance, and operation. In addition, the users of a mainframe computer system tend to be programmers and computer technicians with extensive training.

Since there are many fewer mainframe computers than desktop PCs, there aren't huge libraries of shrink-wrapped programs that can

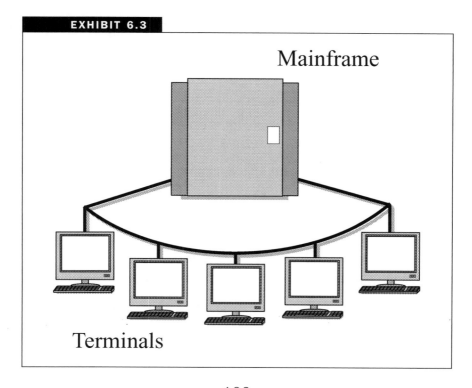

EXHIBIT 6.3

Mainframe

Terminals

simply be loaded and run. Software tends to be proprietary and limited to a few major categories of applications, such as database management systems. Furthermore, because of the processing speeds, the users of mainframe systems tend to be located in close geographic proximity to the systems, connected to the system through a very-high-bandwidth network.

The architecture of mainframe computers is still viable, especially where there is a large amount of data that must be processed very quickly. As hardware designers wrestle with new designs, such as water-cooled units containing hundreds of processors arranged in parallel so that they can perform multiple operations simultaneously, software engineers are at work on creating operating systems that can take advantage of the hardware architecture. The user base for a mainframe computer typically numbers in the tens to perhaps hundreds of users, depending on the capacity of the system. However, mainframes also can service thousands of users by offloading network communications to small, relatively inexpensive, high-performance servers.

The decline of the mainframe as the primary architecture for business computing was due primarily to the availability of integrated circuits (ICs) that made refrigerator-size minicomputers and then microcomputers more attractive on a price-performance basis and in terms of initial investment required. What's more, the virtual doubling of IC capacity every 18 months—the so-called Moore's Law—made desktop systems nearly as powerful as the first mainframe computers.

With the introduction of the desktop microcomputer in the 1980s, computers were no longer acquired by only the top corporations; they now could be a rational business decision for virtually any size business. The electronic spreadsheet changed the perception of the PC from a game machine to a business tool virtually overnight, and PC sales to accountants, small business owners, and corporations skyrocketed. The need for sharing resources rose as well, and every business PC was soon part of a network. Given the local processing power on most desktops in corporate America, a client/server architecture, in which data and other resources are served to a desktop PC—the client—became a viable approach (see Exhibit 6.4). Although minicomputers were used heavily as servers, PC-based servers became increasingly common. The continued proliferation of the desktop PC in the 1980s and 1990s and the availability of powerful servers ushered in the age of the client/server architecture for services ranging from e-mail to corporate decision support systems based on massive corporate databases maintained on high-performance servers.

The client/server architecture is the most pervasive computer architecture in use today. It allows a data server, connected through the Internet or an intranet—whether via cable, satellite, or infrared link—to feed an application running on a desktop PC or other client machine, as shown in Exhibit 6.4. The advantage of the client/server approach is that the management of a database can be performed at a central, controlled location. Furthermore, since database processing is performed on the server and the local workstation or PC handles most of the data manipulation and user interface processing, a single server with modest processing capacity can support thousands of users simultaneously.

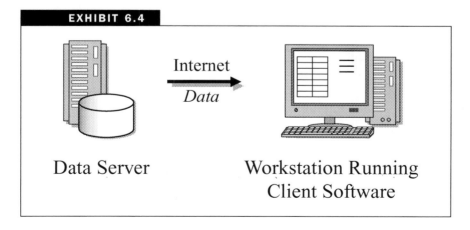

EXHIBIT 6.4

Internet

Data

Data Server   Workstation Running Client Software

The client/server architecture is flexible and affordable, and supports the distribution of data through small local area networks (LANs) and corporate-wide intranets, and over the Internet. One limitation of the most common architecture is that often the software is proprietary. For example, in a corporation with a financial reporting system based on an Oracle database management system, proprietary Oracle client software must be running on the workstation and Oracle server software must be running on the server. Similarly, in order for users to access their America Online (AOL) e-mail accounts running on a AOL server through a dial-up (modem) connection, they must have the proprietary client AOL software installed and running on their workstation.

The traditional client/server architecture probably won't begin to decline in popularity until the middle of this decade, in part because of the installed base of hardware and software. However, there is pressure from the computing industry and consumers for lightweight, affordable, and secure portable devices with extended battery life. There is also demand in corporate America for affordable, small-footprint desktop systems that don't require constant upgrading and software maintenance from the information services (IS) department. The solution to the overhead of maintaining thousands of PCs in a corporate client/server is seen in the general computer industry as Web Services; that is, self-contained, self-described modular applications that can be published, located, and invoked across the web.

Beginning in the late 1990s, the general availability of high-bandwidth connectivity to the Internet and consumers' increased reliance on wireless and portable devices connected to the Internet, as well as software tools based on XML, began steering the computing industry toward Web Services. Unlike the obvious evolution of hardware that accompanied the shift from mainframes to a client/server architecture, Web Services is primarily an evolution of the software infrastructure that relies on a PC running a generic browser instead of a suite of specialized applications.

To better appreciate Web Services, consider that every year, AOL mails millions of CDs of its latest software to potential and existing users, encouraging them to upgrade to the next version of their Internet access and e-mail software. Not only does the mailing cost AOL millions of dollars, but for the consumer or small business owner faced with upgrading their software, it's often a nightmare. During the installation process, it's easy to misplace or erase previous address books, for example, and there may not be enough disk space for the upgrade, requiring users to ignore the upgrade, to spend hours deleting files on their hard disk to make room for the software, or to add more storage capacity to their computer system. The alternative, for users and potential users with a high-speed connection to the Internet, is to simply use the Web version of the program (*www.AOL.com*)—an example of a Web Service.

The Web Services architecture has so many attributes of the traditional client/server architecture that it's probably more accurate to consider it an extension of that architecture. Web Services is a distributed architecture that works over intranets and the Internet and is capable of supporting thousands of users simultaneously. What differentiates Web Services from the client/server architecture is the separation of the data and the data processing functions, including formatting of data for display.

As shown in Exhibit 6.5, in a Web Services architecture, software on the user's workstation doesn't interact directly with the data server. The

EXHIBIT 6.5

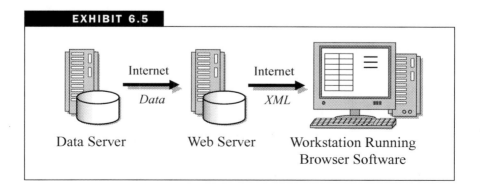

Data Server   Web Server   Workstation Running Browser Software

data are sent instead to an intermediary Web server that performs the processing and formatting. The Web server then sends the processed and formatted data to the user's workstation, where they are displayed in a standard Web browser. The user's workstation needn't have any special application-specific software, numerical processors, or extra RAM (random access memory) installed since the heavy processing is performed by the Web Server. As a result, any computer system capable of running a standard browser environment can access and direct the processing of potentially huge amounts of data. The major impediment, from the user's perspective, is the lack of responsiveness of the system when the network bandwidth is limited. For example, compared to the standard client/server AOL application, checking and composing email through a Web browser over a standard 56K dial-up connection is noticeably slower.

Although an infrastructure based on Web Services is similar to a traditional client/server architecture, it differs in several important ways, as outlined in Exhibit 6.6. The differences are mainly at the top levels of the communications infrastructure, since they both rely on the same physical connections, electrical signals, and network protocols. As shown in the exhibit, data and application layers of the traditional Client/Server model are equivalent to the Discovery, Description, Packaging, and Transport layers in the Web Services model. The lowest layer in the Web Services model, the Transport layer, is responsible for moving XML or XBRL messages between servers to browsers. At the next highest level is the Packaging layer, which is responsible for managing the data exchanged between servers and browsers, including providing a secure connection, enabling digital signatures and other forms of user identification.

Higher in the Web Services model is the Description layer, which is responsible for specifying services, from e-mail to online shopping. This layer consists of XML that describes how services are composed, how they may be moved, how they can interact, and, in general, how they must behave. At the highest layer of the Web Services model is the

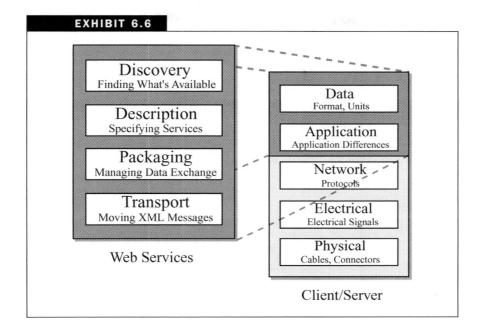

EXHIBIT 6.6

Discovery
Finding What's Available

Description
Specifying Services

Packaging
Managing Data Exchange

Transport
Moving XML Messages

Web Services

Data
Format, Units

Application
Application Differences

Network
Protocols

Electrical
Electrical Signals

Physical
Cables, Connectors

Client/Server

Discovery layer, which provides computer programs with a means of finding what's available. Determining what's available on a PC isn't usually an issue, since software has to be purchased and installed before the computer can be used. In addition, software installation often results in uncertain outcomes. In contrast, with Web Services, there is a potentially unlimited number of different services available, just as a Web search may turn up thousands of potential links to content.

Because the Web Services and Client/Server architectures share network protocols as well as basic physical and electrical standards, they are compatible with the same hardware platforms, from desktop and laptop computers to handheld wireless units. Web Services and Client/Server architectures take advantage of Internet standards to exchange messages, so that any means of Internet transport, from wireless e-mail devices to desktop Web browsers, can be used to view data. Both architectures rely on high-speed networks, whether they're based on fiber, coax, and twisted pair, or wireless.

XBRL Vendors

Although the taxonomy of XBRL will continue to evolve to meet the needs of the financial reporting industry, a number of vendors have announced products that support the initial version of XBRL. Exhibit 6.7 lists a sample of the more notable vendors, categorized by technology platform.

EXHIBIT 6.7

XBRL-BASED REPORTING SYSTEM VENDORS BY PLATFORM

Web Browser

FRS Ltd.	*www.frsolutions.com*
FRx Software	*www.frxsoftware.com*
iLumen	*www.ilumen.com*
KPMG	*www.KPMG.com*
Newtec, Inc.	*www.reportingtools.com*

Windows/Linux

ACCPAC	*www.accpac.com*
CaseWare International	*www.Caseware.com*
eKeeper	*www.ekeeper.com*
Hyperion Financial Analysis Solutions	*www.hyperion.com*
Microsoft	*www.Microsoft.com*
Navision US	*www.Navision-US.com*
Software AG	*www.Softwareagus.com*
XBRL Solutions, Inc.	*www.xbrlsolutions.com*

Database

PeopleSoft	*www.PeopleSoft.com*

In addition to sharing the strengths of the Internet as a communications medium, systems based on Web Services and a Client/Server architecture suffer from the same security threats from viruses, hackers, and malicious or curious employees. Similarly, when wireless devices are considered, encryption and other methods of ensuring the security of messages are required.

XBRL-Enabled Solutions

The increasing popularity of XML-enabled Web Services as an information technology architecture, together with the mobilization of vendors that service the financial reporting industry behind XBRL, portends a future in which solutions to reporting challenges are only the beginning. XBRL is particularly suited for products and services involving communications, data aggregation and syndication, and decision support.

As an enabler of communications between disparate financial computer systems, XBRL can serve as a virtual Rosetta Stone. As illustrated in Exhibit 6.8, corporate headquarters can share data, in the form of XML documents, with a newly acquired subsidiary even though they are using different computer systems, each running a unique operating system, database management system, and reporting software. However, as long as stylesheets are available for translation of documents so that

EXHIBIT 6.8

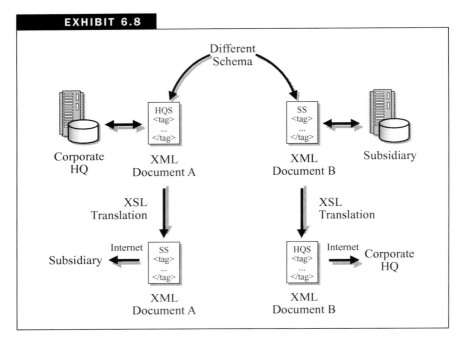

they are compatible with the other system, the documents—and the data they contain—can be shared transparently between the two systems. Stylesheets can be created by end users with high-level editing utilities or purchased from vendors.

Although the system in Exhibit 6.8 is workable, the intermediate translation of XML documents requires computing resources and the periodic maintenance of the eXtensible Stylesheet Language (XSL) documents to reflect changes in the computer system at corporate headquarters or at the subsidiary. A better solution is to use communications based on XML documents that share a schema defined by a standards committee—that is, XBRL. In this scenario, depicted in Exhibit 6.9, the documents exchanged between corporate headquarters and the subsidiary are guaranteed to be readable by the other party, since the documents share an industry-wide schema.

If the computer system at one location is upgraded to a system with a different reporting application, there needn't be any arduous decision

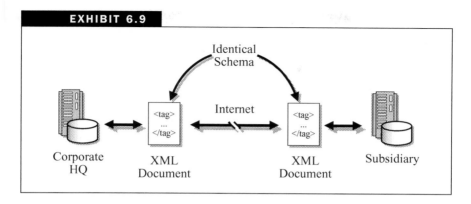

EXHIBIT 6.9

Identical Schema

Corporate HQ

XML Document

Internet

XML Document

Subsidiary

making regarding which of the two IS departments must yield to the other. Instead, both maintain compatibility with the most current XBRL schema. A major benefit of this approach is the ease with which additional subsidiaries can be added to the system without requiring any of the established systems to modify their reporting schema.

The Web Services model, combined with XBRL, lends itself to data aggregation and syndication tasks, where aggregation is the process of collecting data from disparate sources, and syndication is the process of distributing data to disparate channels. A typical data aggregation scenario is illustrated in Exhibit 6.10, where data from any number of Web servers are aggregated into a central XBRL document. The Web servers could be from public corporations, each providing open access to their XBRL-based financial reports. Instead of potential investors and professional analysts reading through each report, an aggregation service combines the numerous reports and, using XML and stylesheets, creates reports customized for individual clients or classes of clients.

The custom reports could be generated on a server and the formatted HTML documents made available on a Web server, or the aggregated XBRL document could be made available to the client, who could then use the local formatting and analysis tools on the data. The former approach lends itself to automatic report syndication, since stylesheets can be developed for alternatives to the desktop PC displays,

EXHIBIT 6.10

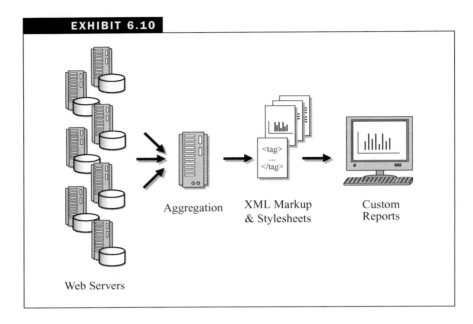

Web Servers   Aggregation   XML Markup   Custom
                                     & Stylesheets   Reports

such as wireless PDAs and cell phones. In this way, the aggregator creates the aggregation system once and maintains a single, up-to-date version of the aggregate XBRL document. If a new model of wireless PDA or panel PC comes on the market, all that is needed is a new stylesheet to describe the unique screen layout characteristics of the device.

An advantage to providing a client with the aggregate XBRL document is that the client is then free to use any number of analysis tools on the data, from spreadsheet-based tools to a variety of statistical analysis tools. Of course, analysis tools that follow the Web Services paradigm are available as well, but a client, such as a large analysis firm, may wish to perform proprietary analysis on the aggregated data and then sell the financial analysis of a market sector or investment portfolio to clients.

Evaluating Potential Solutions

Business solutions are rarely a one-size-fits-all phenomenon, and XBRL-enabled solutions are no different. Solutions must be evaluated in the context in which they will be used. As shown in Exhibit 6.11, the

EXHIBIT 6.11

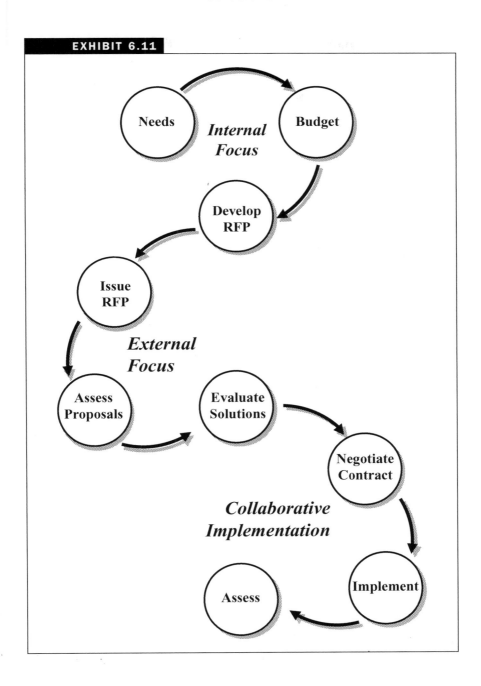

Needs

Internal Focus

Budget

Develop RFP

Issue RFP

External Focus

Assess Proposals

Evaluate Solutions

Negotiate Contract

Collaborative Implementation

Implement

Assess

process of evaluating potential XBRL solutions to financial reporting involves a series of specific steps leading up to the implementation and assessment of the solution. The first phase in the process is primarily internally focused. It includes calculating return on investment (ROI), estimating the corporation's costs in switching to XBRL-based reports, and culminates in a request for proposal (RFP). The RFP represents a consensus within the organization regarding what constitutes an ideal technical solution to the current challenge.

Phase I: Internal Focus

The solution selection process begins with looking inside the business to determine needs, which is where management's knowledge comes into play. Investing corporate resources in a reporting solution that has virtually unlimited internal reporting capabilities may be impressive technologically but may not reflect the practical needs of management.

Internally focused criteria include an assessment of the corporation's information technology infrastructure, price, cultural and technology fit, synergies with existing systems and processes, and risk assessment, as shown in Exhibit 6.12. Unless the IT infrastructure is sufficient to support XBRL-based reporting, attempting to use the technology will likely fail. The infrastructure must include a secure, high-bandwidth network and computers with Web browsers and, when appropriate, XBRL-compatible editing and manipulation tools.

Price is always a consideration in calculating the potential ROI, as is the cost of a failed implementation. Part of the risk involved in implementing an XBRL-based reporting solution stems from internal conflicts with the technology and the cultural changes that it may bring about. For example, although providing management with detailed, customized reports updated daily may sound good in theory, in practice it may lead to inefficiencies or even burnout in managers who normally assess the performance of the people and processes under their steward-

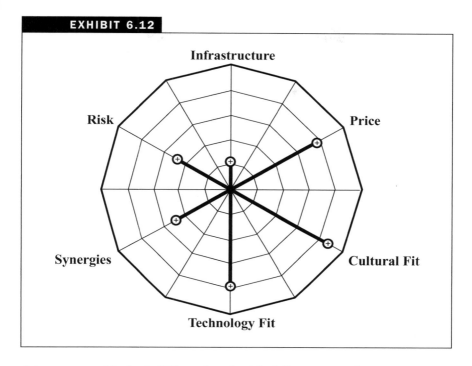

EXHIBIT 6.12

ship on a weekly basis. When faced with daily reports, they may review and act on them daily, to the detriment of other, potentially more important responsibilities, such as spending more time with employees.

Establishing a budget for an XBRL-based reporting project should reflect lost opportunity costs associated with investing the resources elsewhere as well as the costs of staffing and equipping such a project. From a practical perspective, the incremental cost of implementing an XBRL-enabled reporting solution varies from about $100 to $1,000 or more per seat for software alone. Typical additional expenses include an outside consultant and the expense of upgrading the underlying network, support hardware and software, and desktop or hand-held systems. The incremental cost reflects the expense of software licenses, hardware upgrades, and training. In 2003, the annual cost of a networked PC in a corporate office environment was about $5,000 for hardware per seat. A minimal contributor to this figure is the initial cost of the PC amortized over five years. The majority of costs are associated with building and supporting the network infrastructure and acquiring and maintaining software and peripherals.

The third major task in the first phase of the evaluation process is to develop an RFP, a working document that specifies the functional and technical requirements of the technology solution to the current challenges facing the business. Because the RFP is drafted collaboratively, it represents a consensus of opinion inside the business organization. The RFP drives employees and managers involved in the selection of an XBRL-enabled solution to consider the benefits that they expect the system to deliver, as articulated in the requirements specification. Another document driven by the RFP is the functional specification, a technical, detailed description that the system must conform to.

The requirements specification component of the RFP is a qualitative description of the expectations of knowledge workers and managers. In contrast, the technical constraints are defined by the functional specification, which typically includes system software requirements, database software requirements, hardware infrastructure, system capacity, expansion capabilities, installation time line, training requirements, support, and security.

Phase II: External Focus

The second phase in the solution evaluation process is primarily externally focused and leads to the identification of the best solution available that satisfies the constraints defined in the RFP. This phase involves identifying the appropriate technologies and then selecting the developer and vendor that can best deliver and support products that use these technologies. A technologically superior product from a developer with an unrealistic business model or poor reputation is a high-risk investment.

As summarized in Exhibit 6.13, the chief external issues include the overall health of the vendor in terms of its management, market share,

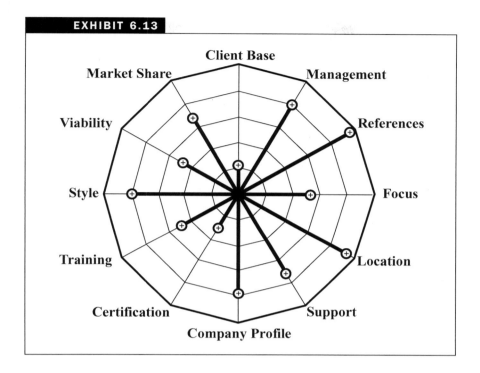

EXHIBIT 6.13

Client Base
Market Share
Management
Viability
References
Style
Focus
Training
Location
Certification
Support
Company Profile

the composition of its client base, references, and focus in the market-place. Additional issues include the vendor's corporate style, relative geo-graphical proximity to the corporation, and type and extent of the sup-port it gives clients. For example, many vendors provide 24×7 coverage via the web, fax, e-mail, and telephone, while others may provide only a modicum of support and only during their normal business hours. The RFP should clearly define the corporate management's requirements for satisfying these and similar issues.

When the responses to the RFP are in hand, the vendors and the solutions they offer should be evaluated on nontechnical, functional issues and on technical merits, as shown in Exhibit 6.14. Criteria include a financial and market assessment of the vendor and developer, the functionality provided by the products under consideration, the fidelity with which they follow the latest XBRL-enabled reporting

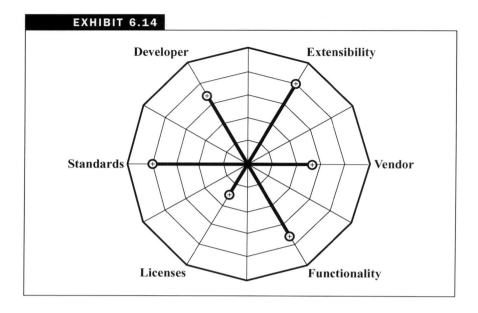

standards, and the extensibility of the products *independent* of the inherent extensibility of XBRL.

Phase III: Collaborative Implementation

The final phase of the evaluation process involves the actual implementation of the solution, from negotiating a contract, to implementing a solution, to assessing the results of the overall effort. After a thorough evaluation of the various proposals from vendors, the next step in the process is to negotiate a contract with the top vendor. Since a vendor's response to an RFP isn't legally binding, it's prudent to fold the original RFP and the vendor's proposal into the final contract.

The second step in the collaborative implementation phase of the evaluation process is to implement the proposed solution. Ideally, implementation is a shared activity that requires external resources from the vendor and the developer and internal resources from the business. Details of the implementation that should be specified exactly in the

negotiated contract include the time line, deliverables, signoff procedure, and means of resolving disputes.

Assessing the results of an implementation involves comparing the
functional and requirements specifications with what is delivered as well
as evaluating the overall effect on the business, especially as reflected in
the bottom line. To this end, Chapter 7 continues the discussion of
XBRL-based reporting from the perspective of the various stakeholders in the financial reporting chain and the likely return on investment.

Technology Adoption

Organizations, much more so than individuals, change slowly, even if
change is obviously the best course of action. The Technology Adoption
Curve, illustrated in Exhibit 6.15, models the time required to achieve
group buy-in for XBRL. The curve can be used to describe the group
behavior of accountants, accounting firms, and their corporate clients.

The shape of the Technology Adoption Curve—an elongated **s**—
can be explained by the statistical quality of variance about the mean of

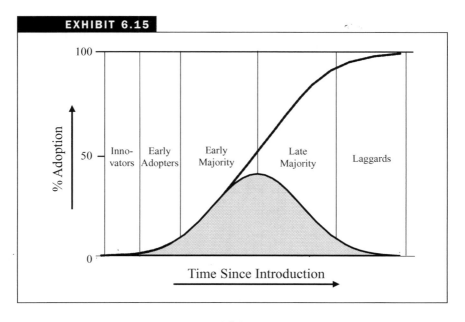

EXHIBIT 6.15

any measure. Many physical characteristics and psychological phenomena, are distributed according to a bell-shape curve, illustrated on the lower half of Exhibit 6.15. Moving from left to right along the bell-shape distribution and counting the total number of adopters along the way results in the s-shape Technology Adoption Curve that extends to the top half of the figure. At the right edge of the adoption curve, virtually everyone in the population of potential adopters has made the change to the new technology.

Marketers in the high-tech industry typically slice the s-shaped adoption curve into five specific areas that describe the characteristics of those in each time slice: Innovators, Early Adopters, Early Majority, Late Majority, and Laggards. The first group to adopt a new technology are the Innovators, who characteristically have an infatuation with the technology for technology's sake. Innovators must have the latest technology, regardless of whether it's practical or provides a solution for a particular problem. That said, Innovators don't necessarily live in the clouds; they may be habitually drawn to new technologies so that they can build on them or apply them in new, nonrelated areas. Often these areas are in an industry that never occurred to the original technology designers. For example, the innovators who chose to use a variant of XML for financial reporting apparently had plans for the technology that didn't occur to the XML designers.

Next along the Technology Adoption Curve are the Early Adopters. Like the Innovators, they are also technology focused, but they are motivated to use the technology to achieve meaningful results in a specific area. Early Adopters don't necessarily mind that the solution isn't plug-and-play and often enjoy the challenge of working with a technology that isn't ready for mass consumption or to perform as advertised. The first users of XBRL fit into this category. They saw the potential of the language in financial reporting applications and weren't discouraged by the ample work that lay before them. Early Adopters are important because they work out the kinks in a technology solution.

A technology is successful or mainstream when it is accepted by the Early Majority. This group of adopters is composed of nontechnical solution-oriented users of the technology. Adopters in this group aren't interested in the nuances of the underlying technology but in what it can do to solve their problem, whether that thrust is to make their lives easier, save time, increase profits, or provide greater value to their customers. The large accounting firms and individual accountants who embrace XBRL-based reporting for the increased efficiency in creating reports and the ability to create custom reports are in the Early Majority.

The Late Majority represents the next most important group of adopters. Like the Early Majority, this group is characterized by a need for a solution that will help them achieve increased efficiency, cost savings, or other practical gains. They differ from the Early Majority in that they may have greater risk aversion, insufficient capital to invest in the technology soon after it is introduced, or greater size and correspondingly greater inertia. They also may be traditionally conservative and resistant to change. For these and other reasons, technology adopters in the Late Majority tend to wait for others to make the first move before committing to change. For their delay and desire for security, they trade a loss in efficiency, cost savings, and other benefits of the technology. There is very little risk in relying on a technology that is in use throughout an industry.

The final group, the Laggards, represent the firms and individuals who change only when they have no other choice. Accountants averse to computers or nearing retirement are likely candidates for membership into this category. Accountants and accounting firms in this category, like those in the Late Majority category, risk losing market share to the competition.

A key question in modeling technology adoption is the time line. Some technology-based products reach the Early Majority stage sooner

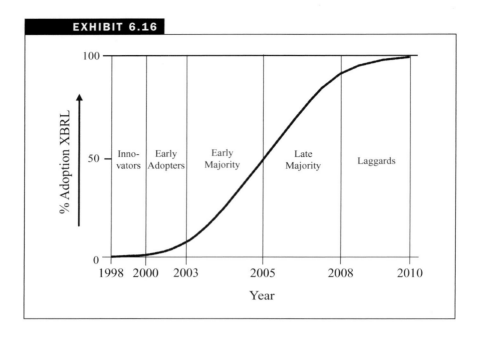

EXHIBIT 6.16

than others. For example, the telephone reached this stage about 75 years after it was introduced, but the cell phone took only about 20 years to reach this stage, and the web, about 8 years. As illustrated in Exhibit 6.16, based on activity in the accounting industry, in 2003 XBRL entered the Early Majority stage of adoption. Due to the widespread acceptance of XML in the computer industry and the leverage provided by the web in deploying XBRL services, the Late Majority of XBRL adopters should begin moving by 2005, with Laggards adopting the technology starting in 2008. By 2010 everyone in the industry should be using XBRL, either consciously or because there are no available alternatives.

Summary

As a solution to the challenge of timely, accurate financial reporting, XBRL is an enabling technology that works synergistically with the current trends in the information technology industry. As the industry evolves from client/server architecture to one based predominantly on Web Services, previously complex operations, such as data aggregation and syndication, data sharing, and the management of data required for corporate decision support, will become virtually effortless for consumers of financial reporting data. One reason for this increase in ease is that Web Services are built with XML, and because its architecture facilitates XML's extensibility, working with extensions of the language, including XBRL, is virtually transparent.

However, even with the synergies made possible by the evolution of IT infrastructures in large and small businesses, it will take time for the industry to embrace the solutions offered by vendors. Furthermore, XBRL-based solutions will inevitably evolve to meet the continually increasing demands placed on the accounting industry, requiring companies that are Early Adopters to update their information systems periodically. Because of these facts, managers evaluating potential solutions to financial reporting should consider not only the technology offered by a particular vendor but the vendor's financial stability, commitment to continued development, and vision in moving forward over the next decade.

Not everything that can be counted counts, and not everything that counts can be counted.

—Albert Einstein

Economics

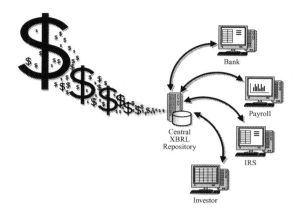

After reading this chapter you will be able to

- Appreciate how an XBRL initiative can yield a positive return on investment

- Appreciate the economic risks associated with investing in XBRL-based reporting systems

- Understand the economic burden of legacy reporting systems

- Identify the hidden costs of XBRL, including the investment in infrastructure technologies that may be necessary to support it

Some investments are necessary for the survival and growth of a business, whereas the value of other investments is less clear. It's intuitively obvious to someone with only a modicum of experience in the manufacturing industry that an automobile factory requires welding machines, conveyor belts, and paint sprayers for the manufacture of cars, for example. However, in the financial information industry,

TIPS & TECHNIQUES

Investing in the Future

Investing in a successful XBRL-based reporting system or other XBRL-enabled technology involves an accurate assessment not only of the company's future requirements but also of the functionality trajectory of the technology. The goal is to satisfy the company's financial reporting and communications requirements without overspending on needless features. For example, consider a product suite offered by a vendor that provides both internal and external reporting capabilities. If the vendor promises advanced internal reporting features in a future version, the product may be overkill for a business interested in a product that facilitates external reporting. In addition, a product that provides a variety of different functionality may be overly complex to learn and use.

Conversely, if management is risk averse and wants to be certain that the product selected will likely meet all future needs, it may invest in a product line that promises functionality far beyond projected need. The premium paid for this level of added future functionality is often viewed as insurance against obsolescence. However, for resource-limited companies, the added cost may be an unwelcome burden.

The key to deciding on an XBRL-based system is to understand the dynamic nature of functionality over time and the parallel maturation of a product along the continuum from magic to a pure technology-based solution. For example, as shown in Exhibit 7.1, a characteristic of functionality is that it tends to increase with time, as a particular technology matures. In addition, the difference between the minimally acceptable and the ideal functionality tends to converge over time, as user expectations rise and as the differentiation between products from different vendors converge.

The challenge in buying in to an evolving technology, such as an XBRL-based reporting system, is to select a vendor and a product with a technology trajectory that falls within the projected needs

EXHIBIT 7.1

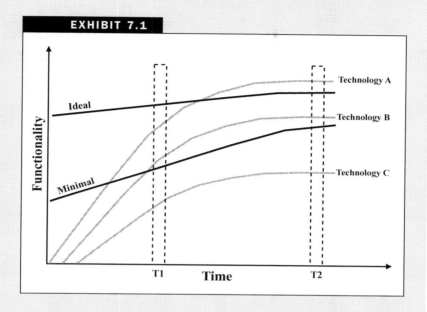

of the corporation without overspending on unnecessary functionality. For example, in Exhibit 7.1, products A and B fulfill the functionality requirements at time T1. However, later, at time T2, technology A provides more functionality than is needed. This isn't necessarily a problem, unless technology A is considerably more expensive than technology B. Technology C never satisfies even the minimum functionality requirements and is a poor investment at any time. Technology C illustrates the case of buying the wrong product early on, with the false expectation that a soon-to-be released update will satisfy users in the near future. In order to select the product with the most appropriate functionality trajectory, in this case technology B, management must understand the company's current and future needs and be able to critically evaluate vendors and the trajectory of their products.

where accountants, financial analysts, managers, and other knowledge workers use data to create other data, it's often difficult to appreciate, much less quantify, the value of a technology that can increase the efficiency and/or effectiveness of communicating, transforming, and otherwise managing financial data.

Even so, few managers doubt the value of timely, accurate information. Satellites relay news and business data from the most remote corners of the world, and the public telephone network encircles the globe. However, data have a cost, and the return isn't always worth the investment. More troublesome is the rate of introduction of new information technologies (ITs) that are resistant to quantifiable return on investment (ROI) analysis because of their short product life cycles and because the investment issues often don't lend themselves to objective analysis.

Consider that in the 1880s, when Alexander Graham Bell first offered his newly patented telephone to businessmen, it wasn't a necessity that could be rationalized by a positive ROI. The telephone was a luxury that allowed managers to monitor the productivity of employees from the comfort of their homes. Similarly, for most of the Japanese businessmen who purchased cell phones in the early 1970s, the technology was more of a status symbol than a device that could actually improve corporate competitiveness. However, in both cases, the technologies eventually transformed the business environment to the point that today many companies cannot operate without wired and wireless communications.

In the case of the telephone, the general business community didn't benefit from the technology until Bell's patent expired near the turn of the century. Then competition pushed the price down to the point where a positive ROI could be demonstrated, and management could accept the potential downside. Similarly, despite the lack of a dependable, nationwide wireless communications infrastructure in the United States, cellular communications are now viewed as a necessity for the traveling corporate executive—and for the line manager walking the shop floor.

As described in Chapter 6, technology adoption is characterized by a number of stages that reflect the perceptions and biases of the potential users, from innovators and early adopters to laggards. However, in working through the economics of XBRL-based reporting, what is most relevant to ROI aren't necessarily the characteristics of the potential user community but the actual, objective, quantifiable status of the technology. One way to understand where a technology, such as an XBRL-based financial reporting system, is in terms of development, is to consider the continuum model, shown in Exhibit 7.2.

The continuum model of new product development describes five key milestones: Inception, Technical Gateway, Product Point, Market Gateway, and Completion. The first milestone, inception, deals with the

EXHIBIT 7.2

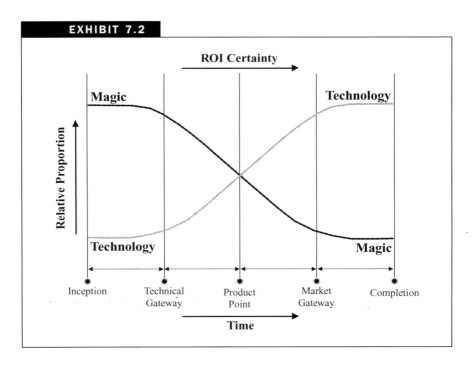

original idea, which might be as simple as a sketch of a product design on a dinner napkin. The second milestone is the technical gateway, which is characterized by a working prototype of the product or process. Next is the Product Point, when a product has completed internal or alpha testing and beta tests using external subjects or consultants is under way. The Marketing Gateway milestone is marked by the appearance of version 1.0 of a product in the marketplace. Numerous technical updates and modifications may be required to finally bring the product to Completion, which marks the end of technical development.

In the Continuum model, significant innovations are initially indistinguishable from magic, in that the mechanism of action is either unknown or a closely guarded secret, repeatability is low, resource requirements are variable, and the results are qualitative instead of quantitative. More important, cost tends to be high, economies of scale are low, the installed base is small, and the ROI is either unknown or variable. At the other end of the spectrum are mature technologies, which are characterized by fixed or low cost, a large user base, a known mechanism of action, high repeatability, and scalability. Most products and services are somewhere between the two extremes of the Continuum model. Determining the position of a product, such as an XBRL-based reporting system, along the continuum is critical to determining the certainty that the calculated ROI reflects reality. Exhibit 7.3 lists internal and external measures for determining when a milestone has been reached in the continuum from idea to product.

The most accurate measures for assessing a product's position along the continuum are based on inside information, such as organizational structure, composition and focus of the management team, planned product enhancements, and the results of internal studies. However, even without internal data, it's possible to assess the position of a product from an external perspective. As listed in Exhibit 7.3, the technical

EXHIBIT 7.3

Continuum Milestones	Internal Measures	External Measures
Inception	Requirements specification written	Informal communications occur
Technical gateway	Functional specifications written; prototype built	Idea demonstrated
Product point	Version 1.0 management team in place	Beta tests run
Market gateway	Product positioned for growth	Market share calculated Competing products appear on the market
Completion	Market focus clarified	Product viability demonstrated Technology improvements made New markets found

gateway typically is marked by the appearance of demonstrations at trade shows, in conferences, and in one-on-one meetings, whereas the product point is characterized by beta testing in the marketplace. In many cases, innovators are sold products that haven't been sufficiently developed and end up playing the role of paying beta testers. In other cases, solution-seeking managers are fooled into thinking that a product is farther along in the continuum than it really is. The market gateway is signified by the availability of market share figures and the appearance of competing products on the market.

Although the management of a company developing a product may not be happy about the appearance of competition, it's a sign that at least one other management team views some aspect of the technology or the approach as a viable business. Finally, the completion point of the continuum is marked by product viability, technology improvements, and the appearance of the product in new markets. Product viability can

Ready for Retirement?

Since the mid-1980s, PC manufacturers have worked under the assumption that the life span of a typical PC in a business setting is about three years. However, since the manufacturing overcapacity following the dot-com bust, many industries are holding on to existing PC systems for four or five years.

Factors that favor the purchase of new computer systems include new, more demanding applications, including new operating systems, a strong economy, a healthy IT budget, and an expanding workforce. The client/server architecture that requires local processing is another pressure for purchasing high-performance hardware. More recently, flat-screen monitors and small-footprint PCs are an incentive for purchasing a new system, especially in settings where desk space is limited or there is a need to project the image of leading-edge technology.

Balancing these forces and restraining new PC purchases are a weak economy, shrinking IT budgets, and a contracting workforce. However, even as the economy recovers, computing is evolving from a Client/Server architecture to one based on Web Services (see Exhibit 7.4). As a result, there is little need to continually upgrade to PCs with more local processing power or disk capacity. As long as a PC is capable of running a standard Web browser over an intranet or the Internet, the hardware is adequate, which allows for a longer replacement cycle.

As the PC becomes simply a commodity item, many PC manufacturers are looking for ways to differentiate their products and increase demand. Aside from physically smaller systems and lower prices, many manufacturers are shifting their focus to manufacturing the servers that provide the infrastructure for Web Services.

EXHIBIT 7.4

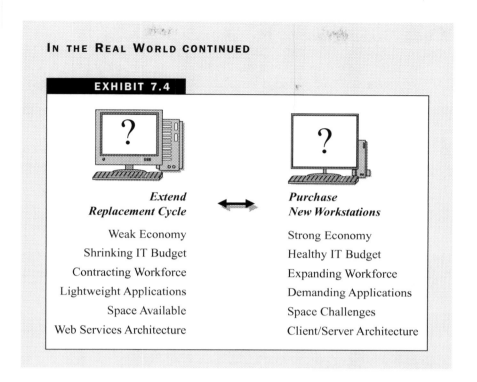

Extend Replacement Cycle	*Purchase New Workstations*
Weak Economy	Strong Economy
Shrinking IT Budget	Healthy IT Budget
Contracting Workforce	Expanding Workforce
Lightweight Applications	Demanding Applications
Space Available	Space Challenges
Web Services Architecture	Client/Server Architecture

be assessed externally through personal communications with other managers, interviewing users, and increased visibility of the product and the developer in the marketplace. Obvious technology improvements, such as new versions, are often highly publicized. The application of existing products in new markets generally isn't attempted until the technology is solid and the limits and potential application to other areas are well known to the management team.

With the concept of the continuum of product development as a backdrop, this chapter explores the economic aspects of XBRL-based products from the perspective of return on investment. In addition to highlighting the economic advantages of the approach, it reveals the most prominent risks, including the need to invest in new infrastructure technologies while maintaining legacy reporting systems.

Value Assessment

The economic potential of XBRL-based reporting varies along the financial reporting value chain. For accounting firms and their clients, the economic incentive to embrace XBRL technology is the potential to increase productivity, enhance work satisfaction, attain a better understanding of client's needs, and, by extension, increase client satisfaction. In addition, by enabling accounting professionals to focus more on consulting and custom reports that suit particular client needs, XBRL-based reporting can help foster collaboration with clients and increase client loyalty. XBRL-based technology also promises time and cost savings over traditional reporting methods. Exhibit 7.3 catalogs the risks and benefits of investing in XBRL technology by area of expenditure.

As shown in Exhibit 7.5, XBRL-based reporting has value that ranges from readily quantifiable cost savings for the corporate accounting depart-

EXHIBIT 7.5

Investment	Value	Risk
Architecture development	Cost savings	Client rejection
Capital	Decreased personnel requirements	Cost overruns
Consultants	Enhanced consulting opportunities	Disruption of service
Contractual obligations	Improved service	Disruptive technologies
Interfaces to legacy systems	Increase efficiency	Diversion of resources
IS support staff	Increased accountant effectiveness	General economic slowdown
Maintenance contracts	Increased client loyalty	Marketplace rejection
Network infrastructure	Increased client satisfaction	Heightened client expectations
PC hardware	Low-level personnel reduction	Inept management
Process reengineering	Time savings	Insufficient technical capabilities
Programming		Poor implementation strategy
Reporting software		Poor system scalability
Software development		Poor usability
Software integration		Rapidly evolving standards
Training		Unexpected costs
Vendor selection		Unexpected drop in demand

ment, the corporation, and the reporting agencies, to qualitative measures such as increased client loyalty. In the former cases, the value is easily measured in dollars, whereas in the latter, it is most frequently assessed in terms of observed client behavior, such as positive referrals and repeat business even in a competitive market. Realizing these cost savings requires an investment in people, technology, and processes. People-oriented investments include training for accountants and others involved in reporting, hiring IT consultants, and the additional information services (IS) support staff required to manage the new reporting system. Technology-related investments range from system architecture development to acquiring new network hardware, personal computers (PCs), and reporting software. Process-oriented investments include changing the roles of accounting professionals and others who author reports.

There is always risk of failure in any business endeavor. As listed in Exhibit 7.5, the potential risks associated with embracing an XBRL-based reporting system range from cost overruns, to unpredictable costs like a general economic slowdown, to technology-related risks, such as poor system or poor usability. Some of these risks, such as a downturn of the economy, can't be avoided. Often the best that can be done in the face of a high-risk scenario is to have a contingency plan in place that defines how the corporation will respond in a new economic environment or to follow a business model that minimizes up-front risk exposure. For example, outsourcing the implementation of an XBRL-based reporting system reduces risk by assuring competency in a new technology. It relieves the company of the need to hire more permanent staff and enables internal staff to focus on their core competencies. Outsourcing also may improve service levels and provide access to the latest XBRL-based reporting technologies. Other risks, such as rapidly evolving reporting standards, can be managed by attention to contractual details, such as provision for timely software upgrades as part of the reporting system software maintenance contract.

Return on Investment

XBRL-based reporting clearly has value for accountants, their clients, and the governmental reporting agencies. At issue is quantifying the value relative to the capital investment required. To this end, the ROI calculation is the most commonly used method of evaluating business performance in terms of earnings returned on a capital investment. Traditionally, ROI is calculated as:

$$ROI = Return/Capital\ Invested$$

where "Return" is the profit, income, or gain and "Capital Invested" is the amount of capital invested during a specified period to produce the return.

The problem with using this ROI calculation with a relatively new technology that has yet to reach the completion stage of the continuum model is that the return can only be estimated. As shown in Exhibit 7.2, the certainty of return is greater as the product becomes more of a technology and less magical.

$$Expected\ ROI = [Certainty\ of\ Return \times Promised\ Return]/Capital\ Invested$$

The major capital investments in the implementation of an XBRL-based reporting system (the people, processes, technologies, and infrastructure) appear in the denominator of the ROI equation. People-related investments include salary, benefits, and expenses for management, consultants, programmers, trainers, and salespeople. Process-related investments include the costs of reengineering, back-end functions, and making license arrangements, while technology-related investments include the costs of new hardware, software, maintenance, security, and customization. Similarly, infrastructure investments include network hardware and software, new facilities, and communications. While capital investments are straightforward, the challenge in an ROI calculation is quantifying the numerator, or promised return value, because of the lack of quantitative results, especially in the short term. Innovation, corporate culture change, and market leadership aren't readily or meaningfully expressed in quantitative terms.

Benchmarking

Benchmarking, using industry- or company-wide best practices as the basis for comparison, addresses many of the qualitative limitations of ROI calculations in establishing the value of an XBRL-based reporting initiative. In a sense, benchmarking is part of every business operation, in that corporate operations constantly are being compared with what successful companies do and earn, and managers want to increase the competitiveness of their organization by learning what other companies are doing. The main limitation of benchmarking is in establishing the value of a new XBRL-based reporting system when there may not be enough hard evidence to link the initiatives of successful companies with their current or future success.

For example, process reengineering was once touted as a means of excelling in business and thousands of companies engaged in some form of it. However, although organizations followed consultant recommendations, the movement failed to provide the results promised. If a particular company had assessed the value of process reengineering by using benchmarking, it may have scored perfectly against the current benchmarks, which would have given the false impression that it was on the path to increased value. However, as it turned out, everyone was striving to be in sync with a flawed program.

Fortunately, several large corporations and governmental institutions have embraced XBRL-based reporting methods, and other companies considering an XBRL initiative could use any one of them for benchmarking. The challenge for management is to identify a company that approximates its size and reporting requirements to use as a benchmark.

Balanced Scorecard

Traditional ROI and benchmarking are lagging indicators, in that they evaluate what happened in the past. These assessment methods provide feedback on past performance but say nothing about how to improve future performance. In contrast, the balanced scorecard technique explicitly establishes objectives, metrics, and indicators. As such, the balanced scorecard technique establishes quantitative and qualitative objectives and how they will be evaluated. The advantage of this approach is that managers know what is required to reach their objectives.

The major limitation of the balanced scorecard approach is that the objectives, metrics, and indicators are defined locally and can vary significantly from one corporation to the next. The manager in charge of establishing metrics and indicators could pick the wrong indicators or too many indicators, or fail to define relevant metrics. For example, in assessing the corporate scorecard, an indicator might be identified as time savings on report generation, with a metric of the number of reports produced per week or month. The objective might be to, say, produce the same number of reports in half the time within a year. However, the number of reports per month may not be the best metric of the relative value of XBRL. A better metric might be the number of requests for custom reports per month, the total time spent by accounting personnel on reporting activities, or the number of hours of additional consulting provided by the accounting group to clients since the implementation of custom XBRL-based reporting. Perhaps the greatest value of the balanced scorecard approach is that it provides a formal mechanism for clarifying how a company can become more competitive in its market.

Time Value

Any assessment of the value of an XBRL-based financial reporting system should consider the time value of the investment in the system. A reporting system is a tangible asset with a finite life span. However, unlike a building or piece of major equipment, the life span of a reporting system is much more uncertain and depends on the acceptance of XBRL in the marketplace and the general financial market.

In some instances, the break-even point for resources invested in a reporting system may come several years after installation. The issue with an extended payback time is that if a corporation invests years of accountants' time in training and the accountants leave the corporation voluntarily or are downsized within a few months, the corporation may not be able to recoup the investment. For this reason, corporations typically limit an early exodus of trained employees by imposing a payback penalty on outside courses taken and paid for by the corporation. However, penalties for leaving the company after in-house training are rarely imposed. Another possibility is that there may never be a break-even point because of changes in the value of the system or because the cost of the reporting system is out of proportion to the potential benefit.

Synergies

For a one-person accounting practice, investing in an XBRL-based reporting package may be as simple as upgrading to the current version of a standard accounting package. However, for larger practices and corporate accounting offices, moving to a new reporting system, or even upgrading an existing system, typically requires a significant commitment of resources from users and support staff. In particular, the IS department may be so intricately involved in any reporting system renovation project that it must be consulted before a purchase decision is made.

Enacting change in the corporate IT environment is usually expensive. It takes time, energy, and money to overcome the inertia of corporate IS culture, especially in larger corporations. Any change has to have not only a reasonable ROI for the intended users, but it should be coordinated with the corporate IS environment. For example, implementing a Web Services architecture in an environment that is fully entrenched in client/server applications is more of a challenge, and likely more costly, than a coordinated move to a Web Services architecture with other IS projects.

The Cost of Intelligence

The cost of business intelligence, whether used for internal control or to comply with externally imposed regulations, is a function of the timeliness, quality, and quantity constraints imposed on the underlying data and, by extension, the reports derived from the data. Returning to the pyramidal model introduced in Chapter 4 and illustrated in Exhibit 7.6, these constraints are mutually orthogonal. For example, increased speed of reporting is typically achieved at the expense of reporting qual-

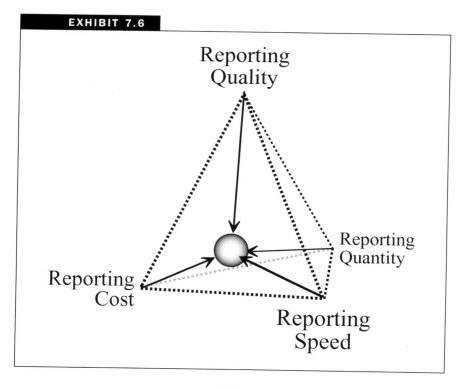

EXHIBIT 7.6

Reporting Quality

Reporting Quantity

Reporting Cost

Reporting Speed

ity. Consider that increased speed generally means that shortcuts are taken and errors are introduced into reports due to carelessness and lack of verification time. The exhibit also illustrates a compromise situation in which cost, speed, and quantity of reporting data are favored over quality, as represented by the area bounded by the sphere near the base of the pyramidal structure.

A technology like XBRL has the effect of contracting and redefining the relative proportions of the pyramidal area defined by the four axes. For example, by replacing an existing financial reporting system with one based on XBRL, an improvement in speed, quality, and quantity of reporting may be obtained for the same cost or even lower cost. The optimum mix of reporting speed, quantity, quality, and cost will be a function of the particular reporting system and the specific reporting requirements. The cost of reports generated on the new XBRL-based system may be greater than that of reports on the old system because of the hardware platform maintenance contract associated with the new system and not because of greater reporting demands per se.

The model offered in Exhibit 7.7 provides another view of how XBRL-based financial reporting can be used to reduce the cost of control reports and generally provide more reports of higher quality, in less time, at a lower cost than would be possible through manual methods. As in the previous model, the relative cost savings attainable through XBRL technology depends on the technology used and the desired mix of data quantity, quality, and timeliness. In this case, technology B, which represents one vendor's XBRL-based reporting solution, provides the same reporting mix as technology A, another vendor's XBRL offering, but at a lower cost. Changing the mix by emphasizing the timeliness of reports, for example, might make technology A the better choice.

Exhibit 7.7 also illustrates several characteristics of technology-based financial reporting. One is that there is a baseline cost attributable to external reporting requirements. That cost represents the resources

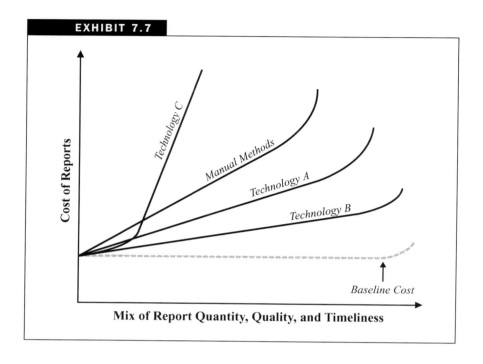

EXHIBIT 7.7

required to assemble and process financial data and distribute them to the appropriate local, state, and federal agencies. Note that the baseline costs associated with reporting increase nonlinearly at some point near the extremes of quantity, quality, and timeliness. There is a similar rise in costs associated with each of the reporting methods illustrated, including manual reporting methods.

The rise in baseline and marginal reporting cost is due to inefficiencies at the fringes of what a particular reporting system is capable of supporting. Especially relevant is technology C, which illustrates the unfortunate but common case of either the use of an inappropriate technology applied to financial reporting or the appropriate technology applied incorrectly to reporting. In this example, the problem is that the technology or process established around the technology doesn't scale very well. There are adequate results when the requirements are minimal, but a higher reporting volume exceeds the capabilities of the technology.

Regardless of the technology applied to data gathering, manipulation, and analysis, at some point the cost of reporting increases sharply for very small improvements in the reporting mix. For example, eventually the maximum information carrying capacity (bandwidth) of the computer network that provides connectivity between disparate divisions of a corporation will be attained. Achieving a higher bandwidth may require tearing out the old cables and replacing them with higher-speed cable and new electronics—often an expensive proposition. Once the new network hardware is installed and operational, however, significant increases in the data mix may be attainable for very small marginal costs. Part of management's charge is deciding when to invest in the new technology in order to achieve the gains possible over the longest time.

Exhibit 7.8 illustrates the relationship between one component of the orthogonal reporting mix, in this case reporting quantity of volume, and ROI. At some critical volume, there is a net savings and a positive ROI. Below that critical volume, there is excess capacity in the report-

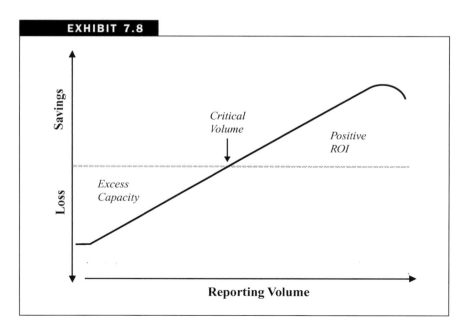

EXHIBIT 7.8

ing system and a loss and a corresponding negative ROI. Above the critical volume there is a net savings in reporting, and a positive ROI. However, as reflected in Exhibit 7.8, eventually inefficiencies become significant and ROI falls. Working at excess capacity is one avoidable cause for operating at a loss. It represents overbuying, either in features or in maximum system throughput capacity.

With the appropriate technology and process in place and appropriately applied, the cost of generating reports can be insignificant when compared with the overall cost of operating the business. Conversely, with inappropriate technology or approach, fulfilling reporting requirements can be a major component of operating costs, especially in smaller businesses.

Exhibit 7.9 illustrates the dynamic nature of technology substitution for a given reporting mix. After the initial investment required to switch from reporting technology A to XBRL-based technology, costs rise less sharply with improvements in the mix. The rate of increase in cost as a

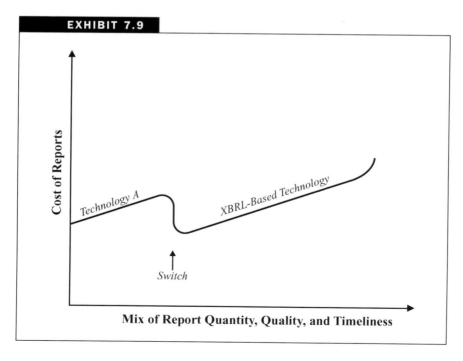

EXHIBIT 7.9

Cost of Reports

Technology A

XBRL-Based Technology

Switch

Mix of Report Quantity, Quality, and Timeliness

function of increasing the reporting quantity, quality, and timeliness depends on the particular mix of these factors and the nature of the underlying technologies. For example, assume that technology A represents a legacy reporting system that is difficult to extend to meet the changing needs of management. Switching to a reporting system based on XBRL provides a much better mix of data quantity, quality, and timeliness than before. Furthermore, the cost of reporting is cheaper. Moreover, it's possible that the new XBRL-based reporting system will drop the fixed costs associated with external reporting to the point that the total cost of the new technology more than makes up for the one-time investment cost of switching reporting technologies.

To better understand how this is possible, consider Exhibit 7.10, which shows the relative reporting costs associated with the legacy system (technology A) and the XBRL-based reporting system. Switching from technology A to technology D involves a one-time investment,

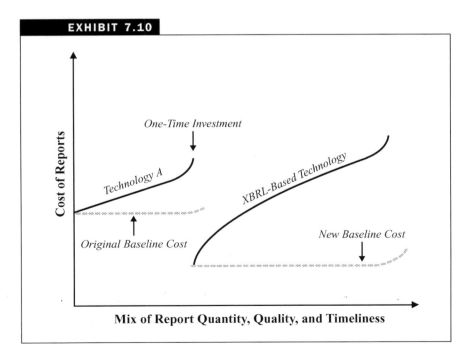

EXHIBIT 7.10

Cost of Reports

One-Time Investment

Technology A

XBRL-Based Technology

Original Baseline Cost

New Baseline Cost

Mix of Report Quantity, Quality, and Timeliness

which is compensated for by the markedly decreased baseline cost. The marginal cost associated with operational reports is unchanged, as indicated by identical slopes of the graphs for the legacy reporting system and the XBRL-based system.

Summary

For most accounting department and reporting agencies, investing in XBRL involves much more than simply ordering and installing a software upgrade to an existing financial reporting package. One complication is that the language is relatively young and many of the products that rely on XBRL are immature. As these products move along a continuum from prototypes to products with a solid technological basis, assessing the value of XBRL-based reporting will be easier and the results of ROI calculations will be more reliable. Although there is clearly value in XBRL and in the process changes that it enables, there are significant risks, ranging from rapidly evolving standards to the appearance of disruptive technologies that may surpass the advantages of XBRL before the financial reporting industry fully embraces the language. The challenge before management is to select the technology solution that provides the mix of quality, speed, and quantity of reporting required by the company, within certain cost constraints. Doing so requires at least a high-level understanding of how XBRL can facilitate reporting, the nature of the reports that must be generated by the system, and, most important, how all of these factors, taken together, affect the company's bottom line.

In business, the competition will bite you if you keep running; if you stand still, they will swallow you.

**—William S. Knudsen,
former president, General Motors**

CHAPTER 8

Are We There Yet?

After reading this chapter, you will be able to

- Recognize the predictors of a successful XBRL-enabled financial reporting initiative
- Appreciate the significance of proper timing in implementing a new financial reporting initiative
- Appreciate and recognize the risks involved in implementing a new reporting system
- Develop a practical implementation plan
- Predict the likely future of XBRL-based reporting and how it will affect your organization

XBRL is a worldwide phenomenon whose time has come. However, until all of the major software vendors incorporate XBRL into their product lines, acting locally requires some individual initiative. Managers who want to use the technology today to position their business for success have several options. They can rely fully on external consultants and vendors, they can work with their internal information services (IS) department to create a custom XBRL-based reporting solution, or they can create an initiative that is somewhere between these two extremes.

Regardless of the approach, there are no hands-off solutions, in that building or buying a new financial reporting system involves many ancillary tasks and considerations. For example, management must weigh the prospect of gain against the risks of failure while considering the timing, corporate culture, and the time and resources to be invested in embracing XBRL-based reporting. Assuming the decision is to move forward, success involves taking action that is aligned with a well thought out and properly executed implementation strategy. To this end, this chapter describes three different implementation strategies for the three major classes of financial reporting entities: large accounting firms, corporate accounting departments, and small, independent accounting firms. First, consider a reality check that is relevant to every information systems project, including the implementation of an XBRL-based reporting system, described below.

Reality by the Numbers

Ever since the computer evolved from the murky swamp of the military establishment and rose to prominence in the business world, there have been arguments over true cost, efficiency, and return on investment (ROI). Stories of multimillion-dollar software and hardware system rollouts that ended catastrophically haunt the chief information officers and other senior managers of Corporate America. For example, despite decades of research into the process of implementing computer-based solutions in the business environment, a full 75 percent of corporate information system implementations result in failure, where failure is defined as a system that doesn't meet the requirements specification established at the start of the project. In many cases these failures aren't catastrophic, but they do require additional time and resources to achieve full functionality.

There are numerous reasons for the high failure rate associated with information system implementations, depending on the nature of the project and the industry. As shown in Exhibit 8.1, the key areas of risk associated with an XBRL-based financial reporting initiative relate to technology, resources, the implementation process, and, most important, the people involved directly and indirectly with the initiative.

Technology

As introduced in Chapter 7, virtually all technologies are associated with some degree of risk, as a function of the degree to which they fail to meet the criteria of a mature technology—fixed or low cost, a large user

EXHIBIT 8.1

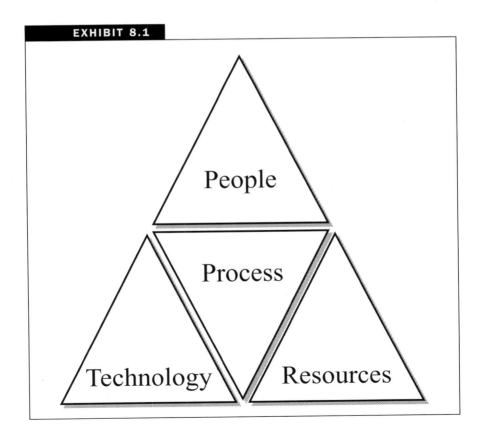

base, a known mechanism of action, high repeatability and scalability. Fortunately, XBRL-based systems meet many of these criteria. XBRL is a free, open standard. Its scalability and repeatability is predicted by the success of XML-based systems, such as Web Services. The general computer industry has demonstrated that Web Services and other systems based on XML are inherently scalable and repeatable. However, there are issues of security surrounding the use of XML and its extensions, XBRL-based systems have yet to enjoy a large user base, and the cost of commercial reporting systems varies, depending on the vendor. Usability is also a product-specific issue that isn't directly related to the selection of XBRL as the underlying reporting language but may be reflected in relatively new reporting applications that haven't benefited from years of use and iterative refinement.

Perhaps the greatest technological risk lies in embracing XBRL as a component of a financial reporting standard. Embracing any standard is risky, partly because there are very few universal "standards." There are, instead, many standards from which to choose. For example, there are several alternatives to XBRL, ranging from proprietary, in-house solutions based on XML or some other language, to other open standards, such as ebXML. Furthermore, owing to XML's ease of extensibility, new alternatives to XBRL may be introduced at any time, just as the standards built around the official version of XBRL will continue to evolve to make better use of the inevitable next version of the language.

Resources

In many ways, business is like a fire that needs a constant supply of fuel to generate heat. The primary fuel for business is capital, both monetary and intellectual, and a new reporting initiative demands its share of both. Many technology projects never make it to completion but remain smoldering for months or years for lack of capital, especially when the launch of a project is undercapitalized. Capital constraints may

IN THE REAL WORLD

Evolutionary Pressure

XBML isn't a clear, uncontested language, even in the relatively narrow field of financial data. For example, although not expressly targeted at financial reporting, ebXML is at least peripherally related to financial transactions; its backers could conceivably extend it to include financial reporting. Similarly, the Open Financial Exchange (OFX) is an XML-based standard for describing bank data and transferring the data over the Internet. The standard used by Microsoft, Intuit, and the banking organizations for information exchange, OFX overlaps with ebXML and, like ebXML, could easily be expanded to include a variety of banking transactions that the accounting industry has earmarked for XBML.

be a result of an internal misdistribution of funds due to organizational politics or because of the general state of the economy. Similarly, insufficient intellectual capital may be a result of failure in the human resources department to hire the people most appropriate for the tasks at hand or due to external factors, such as a general or region-specific labor shortage.

Another resource that is critical for a successful reporting system implementation is a robust information technology (IT) infrastructure. Old, slow personal computers (PCs), an internal network that is poorly maintained, and Internet connections that don't provide for adequate throughput or security are all sources of potential failure.

Process

The process of implementing a reporting system should build on a solid foundation of technology and resources. The appropriate process—a recipe for success—combines the technology and resources in a way that maximizes progress toward the goals established for the reporting system. Even with a mature technology and unlimited resources, without the right process, the risk of failure is high. For example, a process that doesn't include end users, the IS department, and other stakeholders early on is bound to fail. Similarly, the lack of documents defining the requirements and functionality of the new system will likely result in cost and time overruns, frustrated end users and management, and strained vendor relationships. Necessary documents typically include a requirements specification, a functional specification, and a request for proposal (RFP). Additional potential speed bumps in the process include failure to establish contingency plans or a reward system for accountants and others in the organization who must expend extra time and energy to make the reporting system a success.

People

The management and other people who possess the spark that can bring the cold technology, resources, and processes to life are the most important component of a successful reporting system implementation. A successful implementation requires a solid plan—a process definition—and the leadership to bring the plan to fruition.

People at all levels in the organization are critical to a successful implementation and the long-term success of a new reporting system. If end users reject the system's user interface because it's unintuitive or doesn't support the established workflow, or because adequate training isn't available, then the system will fail. Similarly, inadequate or otherwise inept management can quash the enthusiasm of accountants and other end users. Finally, managers who can't operate effectively under conditions of uncertainty or who can't maneuver within the corporate political structure can lose control of an otherwise vibrant, promising initiative.

The following sections continue the discussion of practical issues related to migrating to an XBRL-based reporting system, whether the move is made by small accounting firms, large accounting firms, or an accounting department in a large corporation.

Implementation Process

Regardless of the size and scope of the reporting activity, implementing an XBRL-based reporting system can be viewed as a six-step process that involves Fact Finding, Planning, Resource Allocation, Implementation, Evaluation, and Deployment, as depicted in Exhibit 8.2. As shown, the process begins with Fact Finding, which is concerned with needs assessment, budget, time line, resource requirements, likely return on investment, and a decision on whether to continue with the process and move to the Planning stage.

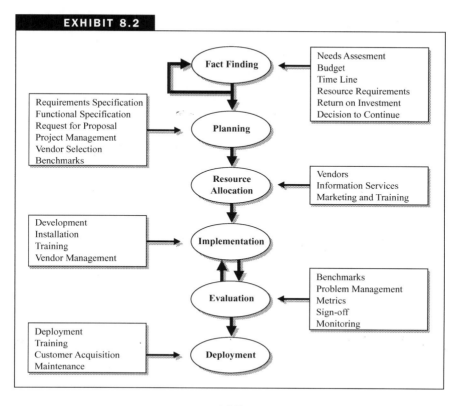

EXHIBIT 8.2

TIPS & TECHNIQUES

Timing Is Everything

Migrating from a proprietary electronic reporting system or a paper-based system to one based on XBRL takes time and requires the coordinated timing of events, whether in a major corporation or a small accounting firm. Relevant questions to ask before making the move are:

- What is the motivation to change now versus six months or a year from now?

- Is the current business model viable without XBRL-based tools and the ancillary activities that the tools make possible? If so, then why change?

- Is there a consensus at all levels in the accounting firm or department that migrating to an XBRL-based reporting system is necessary?

- Is the culture of the accounting firm or department ready for change? If not, what is necessary, other than the simple passage of time, to prepare it for change?

- Is senior management commited to long-term support for standards-based electronic reporting and the creation of ancillary services?

- What are the risks of changing—and not changing—now?

- What is the competition doing?

- What are the lost opportunity costs?

Changing to a new reporting paradigm not only costs the accounting firm or corporate accounting department money and other resources, it also temporarily increases the workload on accountants as they learn the new system. They will learn how to leverage the new reporting capabilities to support high-level consulting and other ancillary activities. In the long term, accountants must learn fundamentally new skills to stay competitive. For accountants near the end of their careers, the return on the time and energy

Planning involves the creation of requirements and functional specifications documents, an RFP, vendor selection, and a formalized project management approach that includes verifiable implementation milestones and contingencies for the inevitable surprises that will be encountered along the path toward deployment. The Resource Allocation phase of the process is concerned with vendors, information services, marketing and training, and other internal resources that must be marshaled for the implementation plan. The actual implementation phase is concerned with development, software and hardware installation, end user training, and vendor management.

The Evaluation phase of the reporting system implementation process is concerned with benchmarks established in the planning stage, problem management, and performance metrics, sign-off on work performed internally and by vendors, and constant monitoring of the process. The Deployment phase is focused on deploying the completed reporting system. Besides placing the system in the hands of end users, deployment involves training, acquiring customers, and the continued maintenance of the reporting system.

The six phases of a typical XBRL-based reporting system implementation process are described in more detail here.

Fact Finding

The goal of fact finding, the first step in the implementation process, is to define the needs of the organization, determine budgetary and time line constraints, estimate resource requirements, and estimate a likely ROI. The end result of this phase is to decide either to progress to the next phase of the implementation process or to wait a specific length of time and reassess the status of the organization and the criteria for moving forward. In performing a needs analysis, the first critical decision for management is to determine who should be asking the questions relevant to the implementation. Politically astute managers involve representative stakeholders in the needs analysis phase of fact finding, as well as in the other stages of the process, by forming of an implementation team. In large organizations, failure to include representatives from IS, accountants and other end users, and marketing in the earliest phases of implementation virtually guarantees failure of the project.

Needs analysis involves identifying the primary stakeholders backing the implementation initiative. These stakeholders should have a major say in defining the implementation timing, approach, and needs that must be met. Besides determining the primary stakeholders, management should have a clear understanding of the political landscape, including dissenters—especially those in senior management. In large organizations, organized labor also may have a say in the implementation of a new reporting system, especially if it means retraining accountants and other employees. The hidden agendas of those in management and labor should also be determined, if possible.

The needs analysis phase should consider the objectives and strategies of those backing the implementation. For example, if an IS department is involved in the implementation process, it should be determined how XBRL and the associated architectures fit in with the department's long-term goals for handling information in the organization. Similarly, the specific reporting and consulting needs of the organization that requires the use of an XBRL-based reporting system should be determined.

Barring in-house technical support, a knowledgeable, experienced consultant can help the implementation committee determine the overall feasibility of the processes, in terms of the budget, time line, resource requirements, and likely ROI. Key feasibility data include the immediate and long-term capital investment requirements associated with the range of possible implementation solutions. For example, quality control comes at a cost, and solutions with little or no provision for quality control may represent a poor value in the long term. The same holds true for implementations that cut back on security measures or redundant systems that can be used for mission-critical processes in the event of massive system failure.

The feasibility of moving to a new reporting system may hinge on the organization's projections of providing additional services to its clients and whether these services warrant investment in an XBRL-based reporting system. In a large organization with hundreds of accountants, migrating to a new reporting system can take years and involve significant restructuring of business processes as well as employee and management relocation and training and a sizable investment in IT. In these cases, the implementation team should determine the projections for growth of the organization, the projected investment in technology, including infrastructure upgrades, custom programming, and managing a legacy system in parallel with the new system until the new system is operational.

Hundreds of unknowns should be addressed in the fact-finding stage, not the least of which is what is possible within the time frame and budget allocated to the implementation team. For example, are there sufficient in-house resources to install or maintain a system? Is the time line for implementation reasonable and compatible with other corporate activities? How will privacy and security concerns be addressed? How will quality control be implemented? What additional training will be required for employees and management, and at what direct and indirect cost? Similarly, of the hundreds of enabling technology solutions, from network infrastructure to servers, which are most appropriate and affordable? Perhaps most important, what are the quantifiable, easily measured indicators of success or failure? A clear, objective standard for success is essential at every phase of the implementation process.

Exactly how fact-finding is performed depends on the culture and size of the organization. For example, external fact finding through site visits can help facilitate external data gathering and provide the implementation team with a perspective on exactly what will be involved day-to-day in an implementation effort. Sending team representatives to attend seminars, networking with colleagues in other businesses, and working with consultants can also facilitate fact finding. Regardless of the approach, senior management must be fully behind the initiative for implementation to move past the fact-finding phase to the planning phase.

Planning

The second phase of the implementation process involves formalizing a comprehensive plan. Key tasks at this phase include defining requirements and functional specifications, creating and issuing a request for proposal (RFP), establishing a project management system, and defining benchmarks that will be used to evaluate the new reporting system. The requirements specifications document formalizes the expectations that management and end users have of the reporting system in terms of benefits, ROI, quality, and service.

The functional specifications document incorporates and crystallizes the requirements specification, the existing and optimal processes in the corporation, industry standards, and the implementation team's vision of the final reporting product. The functional specifications includes technical and process details such as the functional capability of the reporting system, the various software systems employed, hardware requirements, documentation, and provision for maintenance and support.

One of the key tools in the planning stage is the RFP. The RFP should address vendor assessment, pricing, market requirements, functional specifications, development and deployment time lines, licensing and contractual issues, and management's criteria for evaluating each vendor proposal and response schedule.

Planning also involves defining verifiable implementation milestones and contingencies, resource management, and time lines for technology infrastructure improvements, all in the form of a project management system. Optimally, the project management documentation should anticipate the reporting system's life cycle, including the flow of resources and revenue over the lifetime of the system, and anticipate contingencies, including problem management, slips in time lines, and disaster recovery.

It's important to establish benchmarks in the planning stage of the implementation process so that everyone involved in the process, from vendors to management and end users, knows exactly what's expected of them and of the system. Vendors or the IS group will know exactly how their work will be evaluated; management knows precisely what it's committing the organization's resources for; and the accountants are clear on the payback they can expect for training and possible disruption of their normal workflow.

Resource Allocation

The third phase of the implementation process, Resource Allocation, involves identifying and allocating resources that will be needed for the implementation. Resource Allocation is concerned with vendors, IS, marketing and training, and other internal resources that must be marshaled to act on the implementation plan. Vendor relationships are consummated by formalizing arrangements with vendors through contracts, which involves transfer of capital assets to external vendors. Similarly, a relationship with the organization's IS group to provide programming and other services many involve transferring assets within the organization, including employees, furniture, equipment, and intellectual property.

This is also the time to make marketing arrangements with internal and, if applicable, external marketing groups. Internal and especially external marketing requires sufficient lead time to prepare for a campaign. Internal marketing is involved with the initial kickoff meeting, the first official announcement to the accountants and other end users that a new reporting system is being established. External marketing alerts existing and potential clients that new XBRL-based reporting services, as well as ancillary consulting services, will be available soon.

Resource allocation is the time of making provisions for training, using either internal or external training resources. If organizational resources are available, then the training may be internal. In smaller organizations, or in larger organizations without the resources to offer training on the system under development, a contractual arrangement with an external vendor should be arranged. If the reporting system is expected to enable accountants to provide extra-value services, such as consulting, then training of accountants on this aspect of the services offered by the company should begin as soon as possible.

Implementation

The fourth phase of the Implementation Process involves development and/or installation, training, and vendor management. Even in the case where a vendor is used to create a custom reporting system, some internal development is likely to be required to upgrade or at least modify the organization's computing infrastructure. This development may be as simple as installing the latest version of a Web browser on each of the PCs in the organization or as complex as integrating the organization's legacy reporting system with the new system, providing end users with secure access to the Internet, and creating documentation for end users and technical support staff.

Training at least some users on features of the new system also should begin in this phase. Exactly when training should begin depends on the expected duration of the implementation as well as on the likelihood that the system will be developed or delivered on specification and without delays. At a minimum, users who will be involved in the evaluation process should be trained on system operation so that they can provide meaningful feedback to the development group or vendor. Management's role during implementation is primarily oversight of vendors and monitoring the progress of the project based on time lines established earlier.

Evaluation

The fifth major phase of the Implementation Process entails evaluating the results of the first four phases of the process, using benchmarks established in the Planning phase. As suggested by the arrows from "evaluation" to "implementation" in Exhibit 8.2, evaluation also involves iterative problem management. There are inevitably problems in timing, with cost overruns, and in the way resources are managed that adversely affect implementation. Furthermore, evaluation is a continuous process that involves reexamining internally monitored metrics as well as contractual agreements with outside service providers at regular intervals and adjusting the implementation processes accordingly. The goals of system implementation are rarely achieved on the first attempt.

A major milestone in the evaluation phase is signing off on work that has been performed internally or by vendors. However, even if every employee and vendor involved with the project has delivered within functional specification and according to contractual agreements, the resulting reporting system may not work as expected. In this case, the process may need to be modified to reflect the results of the evaluation. For example, the creation of internal operating reports for the central office of a geographically dispersed corporation may be hindered by firewalls—special network devices intend to keep hackers out of the organization's internal computer network. This challenge can be addressed by placing a dedicated server outside of the firewall, opening the firewall for brief periods at certain times of the day, or configuring the firewall to allow communications access between the central office and remote locations.

One of management's responsibilities during the evaluation phase of implementation is to monitor vendor activity to verify that vendors have delivered products and services according to contractual agreements. Evaluation isn't simply a phase that is traversed once; it is a continuous process that involves the reexamination of benchmarks at regular intervals and adjusting the implementation process accordingly.

Deployment

Deployment involves putting the system into the hands of the intended users. Although deployment appears at the bottom of Exhibit 8.2, it is by no means the end of the implementation process. There are recurring issues, such as training new accountants, sales, and marketing professionals; acquiring new customers; and making provision for continuous or intermittent maintenance of the software and computing infrastructure.

Now consider a sample of the more prominent, specific challenges faced by managers involved in three different XBRL-based reporting system implementations—one at a small accounting firm, one at a large accounting firm, and one in a corporate accounting department.

Small Accounting Firm

The process for adding an XBRL-based financial reporting system in a small accounting firm follows the six-phase implementation process outlined earlier. What differentiates an initiative in a small firm from one in a large organization is the amount of time, energy, and personal resources available to research the issues, devise a plan, and then follow through with the implementation process.

The implementation options for a small accounting firm (fewer than three or four accountants) are very limited compared to a large firm with an in-house computer technician or IS department to call on for support (see Exhibit 8.3). Fact finding may be limited to a review of advertisements in the latest trade journals or based on the advice of a paid consultant. Considering that the cost of a financial reporting sys-

---

EXHIBIT 8.3

SMALL ACCOUNTING FIRM IMPLEMENTATION ISSUES	
Fact finding	Limited resources and time
	No IS department
	Limited to shrink-wrap options
	Usually involves external consultants
Planning	Should consider disruption of business operation
	Arranging accountant training
Resource Allocation	Availability of capital
Implementation	May involve upgrading infrastructure
Evaluation	Parallel legacy operation period
Deployment	No internal technical support

tem for a small firm can run anywhere from $100,000 and up, spending a few thousand dollars on a consultant can be a good investment.

Because the number of users is limited, the planning and resource allocation steps tend to be short, direct, and driven by need instead of politics. Since there is a limited number of accountants and support staff, everyone tends to be involved in the implementation process, which often results in a disruption of business operations. Resource allocation is typically a matter of writing a check to a consultant or external vendor, since there is no IS department or other internal organization to deal with. Similarly, the implementation phase of the process tends to be short, unless there is need for some custom programming or the installation of a new computer system or other component of the supporting infrastructure.

The evaluation phase tends to be short as well, because the firm's three or four accountants can evaluate a system and easily communicate their findings to each other. To avoid total dependence on the new, unproven system, there is often an initial period during which the old system is available and operational, even if only on one PC that must be shared by all staff members. Finally, deployment needn't be accompanied by an extensive internal marketing campaign, since everyone in a small office will be aware of the progress of the implementation.

The main issue with the implementation of any new reporting system in a small accounting firm is making time for training so that productivity-related losses are kept to a minimum. For example, there may be only a handful of PCs in the firm, and if every one is being upgraded to a new system, the office is at a standstill until the installation is finished. Practical solutions involve making the final installation on weekends and not attempting to switch over to a new reporting system at the height of tax season.

An overriding issue with a small group practice moving to an XBRL-based reporting system is planning for time off for all accountants to attend courses or otherwise learn about interpreting the custom reports that they will market to their clients. That is, they have to learn a new set of skills to be competitive in the new financial reporting marketplace.

Large Accounting Firms

With size comes complexity, and the large accounting firms with upward of hundreds of accountants on staff, dedicated IS departments, and small armies of support staff are as complex an environment as it gets for the implementation of a new financial reporting system. Exhibit 8.4 lists some of the key issues characteristic of implementing an XBRL-based reporting system in a large accounting firm.

One of the advantages of a large organization is typically the ready availability of personnel and other resources. The fact-finding phase of the implementation process is facilitated by access to representatives throughout the organization to serve on the implementation team. One of the most important members of this team is the representative from the IS department. This representative is especially critical if, in the course of planning, the decision is made to build all or part of the system instead of working with a vendor or purchasing a shrink-wrapped solution.

EXHIBIT 8.4

LARGE ACCOUNTING FIRM IMPLEMENTATION ISSUES	
Fact finding	Implementation team members
	IS department involvement
Planning	Buy versus build
Resource Allocation	External marketing and sales
Implementation	System training
	User documentation
Evaluation	Implementation team benchmarks
Deployment	Internal and external marketing
	External sales

A key issue with resource allocation within a large accounting firm is the necessary focus on external marketing and sales. Although there should be some internal marketing throughout the organization, the primary marketing focus is on external clients. Because there may be dozens of end users, system training for end users and user documentation should be created during the implementation phase of the process. Evaluation of XBRL-based reporting systems is generally based on a comparison of system performance and features with the benchmarks established by the implementation team members. Finally, deployment within a large accounting firm typically requires internal and external marketing efforts as well as external sales.

Corporate Accounting Departments

The complexity of implementing an XBRL-based reporting system in a corporate accounting department falls somewhere on the scale of difficulty between small and large accounting firms. The overall organizational structure may be more or less complex than that of a large accounting firm, depending on the industry in which the corporation operates. For the most part, the issues faced by management in the corporate accounting department are identical to those faced by management in large accounting firms. The main differences are more in degree rather than in kind.

For example, as shown in Exhibit 8.5, the corporate accounting office may be considered a burden by the IS group, which may be concerned primarily with other challenges in the organization. In contrast, a large accounting firm typically has a dedicated IS group. One of the major distinctions of the reporting system implementation process for corporate accounting departments is that there is no need for external marketing. Since there are no outside clients, marketing is limited to internal accountants and support staff.

Regardless of the size of the implementation, and regardless of whether the environment is a corporate accounting department in a

EXHIBIT 8.5

CORPORATE ACCOUNTING DEPARTMENT SPECIFIC ISSUES	
Fact finding	Identifying stakeholders
Planning	Implementation team selection
Resource Allocation	Internal marketing and training
Implementation	Employee training
	Employee documentation
Evaluation	Implementation team benchmarks
Deployment	Internal marketing

Fortune 500 company or a five-person accounting firm, predictors for success are virtually identical, as described below.

Predictors of Success

In alignment with Yin and Yang, the classic principle of opposites, the predictors of a successful implementation are based on the same factors that represent the greatest risks for failure: technology, people, process, and resources (see Exhibit 8.6). The most important factor, people, starts with management. Effective managers are able to articulate a clear, shared vision for the organization, to make the accountants and others involved in the project aware of the potential benefits of an XBRL-based reporting system, and to impress on them the need to change. Since a realistic implementation time line for a full-featured XBRL-based financial reporting initiative can range from several months for a department-wide implementation to a year or more for corporations whose physical plants are distributed around the globe, keeping the vision in front of every employee can be a major challenge.

Technology can help in maintaining contact with the leadership. Infrastructure technologies enable XBRL-based reporting systems to be installed and operated with minimal difficulty and disruption to the operation of the organization. From a process perspective, implement-

EXHIBIT 8.6

ing a reporting system in such a way as to ensure consistency, simplicity, and structure adds to the prospects of success. Finally, strategic utilization of resources as well as strategic partnerships go a long way toward ensuring a successful implementation.

Effective change managers can galvanize a capable workforce behind a clear vision that simultaneously moves everyone toward individual goals and toward the collective goals of the organization. That is, successful managers lead by pulling others along. Unsuccessful managers merely manage, prodding everyone along, and constantly have to stop and deal with stragglers and those who have wandered off the ever-changing path.

Successful managers also embrace an implementation plan that involves feasibility assessments, strategic planning, and continued assessment, and manage risk through contractual agreements, redundant reporting systems, and provision for multiple contingencies. They also know when to accept added responsibilities and when to outsource components of the implementation to knowledgeable, experienced outside consultants. Perhaps the greatest challenge accounting and IT professionals face is proving to investors, senior management, and other primary stakeholders that investing in XBRL-based methods will result in a significant, quantifiable increase in the value of the organization.

On the Horizon

Nothing takes the past away like the future, and the future of XBRL is interoperability with other XML-based systems and other information technologies such as wireless and data security. Eventually these technologies will support operational reports for managers that include real-time data from the point of sale or that results from other business transactions. Technologies that allow for real-time inventory assessment, detect shrinkage, follow products in transit, and acquire other real-time data are becoming commonplace and eventually will be fully integrated into the XBRL-based reporting systems. This level of integration assumes continued growth in technologies such as Web Services as well as in technologies just over the horizon, such as Grid computing, which will bring supercomputer power to desktop and hand-held devices.

What does this portend for an organization? It means that more data and more processing power will be available to managers than ever before. The common challenge of managing in a realm of uncertainty will soon be transformed into a challenge of deciding what data to focus on and what data to ignore. For accounting professionals, this proliferation of data represents a unique, once-in-a-lifetime opportunity to redefine the profession as they take on more consultative roles in their relationships with clients.

Summary

XBRL-based financial reporting is here, but not yet in the form of a shrink-wrapped software package that can be purchased at a corner computer supply store. However, for managers who want to enjoy the potential benefits of the technology today, there is a process for moving forward. The process, which involves Fact Finding, Planning, Resource Allocation, Implementation, Evaluation, and finally Deployment, is virtually identical for small or large accounting firms or corporate accounting departments. In each case, the predictors of success—and failure—are technology, resources, process, and people.

As in every IT endeavor, technology alone is of little value to the organization without the resources, processes, and people to bring it all together in the form of a reporting system that fulfills everyone's needs. Clearly, there are risks associated with embracing XBRL today, but the risks of ignoring the information revolution that has transformed virtually every form of business on the planet are even greater. Regardless of whether the current version of XBRL becomes the universal language for financial reporting, its very presence is permanently redefining the nature of the accounting field and the expectations of reporting agencies worldwide.

Nobody can really guarantee the future. The best we can do is size up the chances, calculate the risks involved, estimate our ability to deal with them and then make our plans with confidence.

—Henry Ford II, former chairman,
Ford Motor Company

Glossary

Application A software program that supports a specific task, such as word processing.

Architecture The general technical layout of a computer system.

Back-end process A process that doesn't represent a company's unique skills, knowledge, or processes. Typical back-end processes include payroll, billing, and accounts payable.

Bandwidth A measure of the information-carrying capacity of a medium.

Benchmarking A method of comparing contracted services to services delivered.

Best practice The most effective and desirable method of carrying out a function or process.

Browser A software program that interprets documents on the web. Netscape Navigator and Microsoft Explorer are the two most popular browsers in use today.

Client/Server A computer architecture in which the workload is split between desktop PCs or hand-held wireless devices (clients) and more powerful or higher-capacity computers (servers) that are connected via a network such as the Internet.

Controlled vocabulary A terminology system unambiguously mapped to concepts.

Data mining The process of extracting meaningful relationships from usually very large quantities of seemingly unrelated data.

Data warehouse A central database, frequently very large, that can provide authorized users with access to all of a company's information. A data warehouse usually is provided with data from a variety of noncompatible sources.

Database management system (DBMS) A system to store, process, and manage data in a systematic way.

Decision support system Software tools that allow managers and other knowledge workers to make decisions by reviewing and manipulating data in a data warehouse.

Disruptive technology A technology that empowers a different group of users and gets better over time. The PC was a disruptive technology, in that it empowered individuals to perform tasks once relegated to large data centers.

Early adopter In marketing circles, a customer who wants the latest and greatest gadget, regardless of cost or inconvenience.

Ease of use Regarding a user interface, the ease or efficiency with which the interface can be used. An easy-to-use interface may be difficult to learn and vice versa.

ebXML Electronic Business eXtensible Markup Language is an evolving XML-base standard for doing business over the Internet. Unlike XBRL, which is concerned with historical reporting of financial data, ebXML is transaction oriented and is intended to encompass all business operations.

Electronic data interchange (EDI) A standard transmission format for business information sent from one computer to another.

Element A triad of opening tag, text, and closing tag in an XML document.

Encryption The process of encoding data to prevent people without the proper key from understanding the data, even though they may have access to the data.

Enterprise resource planning (ERP) The category of software designed to improve the internal processes of a company.

Expert system A type of computer program that makes decisions or solves problems in a particular field by using knowledge and analytical rules defined by experts in the field.

Extensible Stylesheet Language (XSL) A language that applies element formatting rules for an XML document. It can transform the structure of the document, amalgamate several documents into one document, or produce several documents from a single XML source file. It contains functions for formatting, sorting, concatenating, condition testing (if-then), logical operations (and, or, not), and mathematical operations (sum, round).

Functional specification A document that incorporates and crystal-lizes the requirements specifications and specifies exactly what a software and/or hardware system will deliver.

Generally accepted accounting principles (GAAP) The conventions, rules, and procedures that define accepted accounting practice, as defined by the Financial Accounting Standards Board (FASB).

Great Global Grid (GGG) The next-generation web, which provides access to processing power and software resources on demand.

Infrastructure In the context of information technology, the system of servers, cables, and other hardware, together with the software that ties it together, for the purpose of supporting the operation of devices on a network.

Intellectual property Know-how, trade secrets, copyrights, patents, trademarks, and service marks.

Interface The procedures, codes, and protocols that enable two systems to interact for a meaningful exchange of information.

Internet *An* internet is a collection of local area networks (LANs) connected by a wide area network (WAN). *The* Internet is the World Wide Web, one of many internets.

Java A programming language developed by Sun Microsystems used in Web development.

Knowledge management A deliberate, systematic business optimization strategy that selects, distills, stores, organizes, packages, and communicates information essential to the business of a company in a manner that improves employee performance and corporate competitiveness.

Knowledge workers Employees hired primarily for what they know.

Knowledgebase A database that contains information about other data contained in the database. The data or information needn't reside in a traditional database management system to be considered a knowledgebase.

Legacy system An existing information system in which a company already has invested considerable time and money. Legacy systems usually present major integration problems when new, potentially incompatible systems are introduced.

Metalanguage A language used to define other languages.

Object oriented A system based on independent, self-contained program or data structures that are hierarchically related.

Personal digital assistant (PDA) A personal, hand-held organizer. The Palm Pilot is the quintessential PDA.

Reengineering The process of analyzing, modeling, and streamlining internal processes so that a company can deliver better-quality products and services.

Request for proposal (RFP) A document that requests prospective service providers to propose the terms, conditions, and other elements of an agreement to deliver specified services.

Requirements specification A description, in operational terms, of what management expects the vendor's product or service to do for the company.

Return on investment (ROI) Profit resulting from investing in a company, process, or activity. The profit could be money, time savings, or other positive result.

Schema A document that defines the rules for the structure and the content of an XML document. The schema acts like a template within the document that specifies the form that the XML document must take. Schemas work better with data that must follow a particular structure. A schema can specify decimal, integer, date, and time formats.

Server A computer that controls access to the network and net-based resources.

Standards Agreed principles of protocol set by government, trade, and international organizations that govern behavior.

Stylesheet A file that defines how XML data should appear.

Syntax The ordering of and relationship between the words and other structural elements in phrases and sentences.

Systems integration The merging of diverse hardware, software, and communications systems into a consolidated operating unit.

Taxonomy The classification of concepts and objects into a hierarchically ordered system that indicates relationships.

Template The instructions in an XSLT stylesheet that control how an element and its content should be changed.

Value chain The sequence of events in a process that adds value to the final product or service.

Web Service A tool or capability that can be accessed through the web rather than being run locally on a desktop.

Web Services An XML-based interface specification for distributed software to communicate over a network.

World Wide Web Consortium (W3C) The working group responsible for XML specifications. The goal of the W3C is to develop interoperable technologies (specifications, guidelines, software, and tools) to lead the web to its full potential.

Further Reading

Books

Eckstein, R., and M. Casabianca. *XML Pocket Reference*. Sebastopol, CA: O'Reilly & Associates, 2001.

Kotok, A., and D. Webber. *ebXML: The New Global Standard for Doing Business over the Internet*. Indianapolis: New Riders, 2002.

Ray, E. *Learning XML*. Sebastopol, CA: O'Reilly & Associates, 2001.

Rumizen, M. *The Complete Idiot's Guide to Knowledge Management*. New York: Alpha Books, 2001.

Silbiger, S. *The Ten Day MBA*. New York: William Morrow and Company, 1999.

Simon, S. *XML*. New York: McGraw-Hill, 2001.

Standefer, R. *Enterprise XML Clearly Explained*. New York: Morgan Kaufman, 2001.

Tracy, J. *The Fast-Forward MBA in Finance*. New York: John Wiley & Sons, 1996.

Periodicals

Journal of Accountancy

Strategic Finance: www.strategicfinancemag.com

XML & Web Services: *www.xml-mag.com*

Web Sites

CFO.com: *www.cfo.com*

Cover Pages: *www.oasis-open.org/cover/xbrl.html*

Morgan Stanley: *www.morganstanley.com/xbrl/*

Open Financial Exchange: *www.ofx.net*

PriceWaterhouseCoopers: *www.pwcglobal.com*

U.S. Securities and Exchange: *www.sec.gov*

World Wide Web Consortium (W3C): *www.w3.org*

XBRL Express: *www.edgar-online.com/xbrl/*

XBRL Home Page: *www.xbrl.com*

XBRL Public: *groups.yahoo.com/group/xbrl-public/*

XBRL Resource Center at Bryant College:
www.Bryant.edu/~xbrl/index.html

Index

Genome Annotation Markup
    Elements (GAME), 114
GGG (Great Global Grid), 205
GML (Generalized Markup
    Language), 107
Gracenote CDDB Music
    Recognition Service, 126
Grammar, 109
Graphical user interface (GUI), 108
Great Global Grid (GGG), 205

H

Healthcare industry, 3–4
Health Level 7 (HL7) protocol, 3
Heraclitus, 27
Hewlett-Packard, 18
High-bandwidth connectivity, 136
HL7 (Health Level 7) protocol, 3
HTML, *see* Hypertext Markup
    Language
Human resources, 84
Hypertext Markup Language
    (HTML), 8, 9, 108, 114–116

I

IBM, 18
ICs (integrated circuits), 134
Implementation:
    assessing benefits of, 6–7
    collaborative, 150–151
    time frame for, 25
Implementation process, 185–201
    corporate accounting department
        example of, 198–199
    deployment phase of, 187–188,
        194–196, 198
    evaluation phase of, 187, 193–194,
        196, 198
    fact finding phase of, 185,
        188–190, 195–197
    implementation phase of, 187, 193,
        196, 198

large accounting firm example of,
    197–198
planning phase of, 187, 190–191,
    196–197
predictors of successful, 199–201
resource allocation, 187, 192, 196,
    198
small accounting firm example of,
    195–197
timing of, 186–187
Implementation team, 188
Inception (of new product develop-
    ment), 161–162
Incremental cost, 147–148
Information (definition), 22
Information systems, failure rate of,
    180
Information technology (IT):
    changing nature of, 24–25
    infrastructure evolution of,
        130–139, 141
    and standards, 53–54
Infrastructure, 130–141
    client/server, 134–139, 141
    definition of, 205
    investments in, 168
    mainframe, 131–134
    PC, 134–135
    as resource, 183
    Web services, 136–139, 141
Innovation, 82–83
Innovators, 152
Insourcing, 45
Integrated circuits (ICs), 134
Intellectual capital, 183
Intellectual property, 205
Intelligent agents, 97, 105–107
Interfaces:
    definition of, 205
    and size of system, 45–46
    system, 4–5, 7–10

Internally focused evaluation criteria, 146–148

Internal marketing, 192, 198

Internal reports, 3

Internal Revenue Service (IRS), 35, 108

International financial standards organizations (list), 16

International Organization for Standardization (ISO), 108

International Telecommunications Union Telecommunications Standardization (ITU-T) standards, 4

Internet, 57, 97, 108, 139, 205

Internet-based reporting, 13–15, 39–41, 105

Intuit, 183

IRS, *see* Internal Revenue Service

ISO (International Organization for Standardization), 108

IT, *see* Information technology

ITU-T (International Telecommunications Union Telecommunications Standardization) standards, 4

J

Japanese Article Number (JAN), 20

Java, 110, 112, 116, 205

K

KM, *see* Knowledge management

Knowledge base, 205

Knowledge (definition), 22

Knowledge management (KM), 79–80, 92–96, 205

Knowledge workers, 205

Knudsen, William S., 178

L

Labor, organized, 188

Laggards, 153

Language(s), 109–113

computer, 109–113

declarative vs. procedural, 109–111

definition of, 109

object-oriented programming, 111–113

LANs (local area networks), 136

Large accounting firms, 197–198

Late Majority, 153

Legacy systems, 25–26, 205–206

Libraries, 102–104

Life span (of technology), 164–165, 171

Linux, 18

Local area networks (LANs), 136

Lost opportunity costs, 186

Lower-level managers, 83

M

Macintosh (Apple), 108

Mainframe computers, 131–134

Management, 80–86

and benchmarks, 191

and communications, 83–84

compromises of, 85–86

and data overload, 81–82

and evaluation phase, 194

and implementation phase, 193

and innovation, 82–83

and people-oriented investment, 184

successful, 200–201

Management control data, 84

Marketing, 192, 198

Marketing gateway (of new product development), 162, 163

Markup (term), 104

Metadata (definition), 22

Metalanguage, 206

Metcalf, Bob, 54

Metcalf's Law, 54

Microcomputers, 134

X

XBRL, *see* eXtensible business reporting language

XBRL-enabled solution evaluation, 144–151

collaborative implementation phase of, 150–151

external focus phase of, 148–150

internal focus phase of, 146–148

Xerox, 108

XFRML (Extensible Financial Reporting Markup Language), 108

XML, *see* eXtensible Markup Language

XML-MTF (Extensible Markup Language—Message Text Format), 114

XSL, *see* Extensible Stylesheet Language

X.12 standard, *see* American National Standards Information X.12 standard